American Folk Art

for **Kids**

with 21 Activities

R I C H A R D   P A N C H Y K

CHICAGO REVIEW PRESS

Library of Congress Cataloging-in-Publication Data
Is available from the Library of Congress.

©2004 by Richard Panchyk
First edition
Published by Chicago Review Press, Incorporated
814 N. Franklin Street
Chicago, Illinois 60610

ISBN 1-55652-499-4

Printed and bound in China
5 4 3 2 1

Cover and interior design: Joan Sommers Design

Art and Photo Credits

Page vii Bill Traylor, *Untitled*, ca. 1940. Photograph courtesy of Judy A. Saslow Gallery, Chicago

Page ix, 13, 16, 18, 19, 22, 26 (bottom), 38 (bottom), 40 (center and right), 42 (left), 54, 57, 66, 69 (right), 72, 75 (left), 77, 80, 82, 87, 92, 95, 104, 106, 108 by Richard Panchyk

Page 4, 19, 26 (top), 38 (top), 40 (left), 46, 47, 49, 58, 69 (left), 71, 73, 74, 78, 79, 83, 84, 89, 90, 93 (right), 94, 98, 111 by Frank Iraggi

Page 14, 62, 76, 103 copyright Schecter Lee/Esto

Page 5, 56 (left), 64 by Elina Leonova

Page 33, 91 by Jerome Pohlen and James Frost

Page 42 (top) by Caren Prommersberger

Page 3 by Joan Sommers

Page 20 Grandma Moses, *Sugaring Off*. Copyright 1946 (renewed 1974) Grandma Moses Properties Co., New York

Page 24 Edward Hicks, *Peaceable Kingdom*, ca. 1848, oil on canvas, overall: 23 7/8 x 31 7/8 (60.64 x 80.96 cm), Albright-Knox Art Gallery, Buffalo, New York, James G. Forsyth Fund, 1940

Front cover images (clockwise from right): Tin man, 1994, collection of Jerome Pohlen and James Frost; Toy village with church and houses, mid-20th century, collection of Frank Iraggi; Painting of a bird and flowers, mid-20th century, collection of Richard Panchyk; David Butler, *Monster Whirligig*, ca. 1968, cut tin, enamel, and wood, 23 x 24 x 35, John Michael Kohler Arts Center permanent collection; Detail of crazy quilt, late 19th or early 20th century, collection of Elina Leonova; Painting of a girl with flowers, attributed to William Matthew Prior, 1830–1850, copyright Schecter Lee/Esto.

Back cover images (clockwise from top right): Elijah Pierce, figure of Abraham Lincoln, ca. 1975, carved and painted wood, copyright Schecter Lee/Esto; Marvin W. Blodgett, two panels of painting of deer, ca. 1960, reverse painting on glass truck window, collection of Joan Sommers; Bill Traylor, *Untitled*, ca. 1940. Photograph courtesy of Judy A. Saslow Gallery, Chicago; Duck decoy, artist unknown, Wisconsin, early 20th century, collection of Joan Sommers; Peter Prommersberger, Whirligig, 1990, collection of Frank Iraggi.

For Elizabeth

Contents

First and foremost, very special thanks to William C. Ketchum Jr., for sharing his vast wealth of knowledge about folk art, for reading over the manuscript, and for helping steer me down the right path. This book would not have been possible without his guidance.

Also, very special thanks to Mr. Imagination for taking the time to share his art and ideas with me. His dedication to educating kids about art is inspiring.

Thanks to Beverly Finster and Hildegard Bachert for taking the time to talk with me. Thanks to Brother Arnold and the Sabbathday Lake Shaker Community for answering my questions. Thanks to Frank Iragqi and Elina Leonova for taking some excellent photographs. Thanks to Peter Prommersberger for sharing his art works.

Thanks to Willy Heilmann for taking me to the Ivory Museum in Erbach and sharing his collection with me. Also thanks to the following people who helped me in the course of my research: Eva Arvai, Msgr. Donald Sakano, Roger Nancoz, Ruth Sellons, Norman Giradot, Rose Mary Vincent, Kirsti Bloom, Eleanor Sullivan, Axel Uhrig. Thanks to the Windsor Historical Society in Connecticut for providing some needed information. Thanks to Oster-Jensen Antiques in Locust Valley, New York, for access to their folk art.

Thanks also to my wife, Caren, for her editorial skills, and to Caren, Matthew, and Elizabeth for their patience and understanding. Also thanks to my excellent editors at Chicago Review Press, Cynthia Sherry and Jerome Pohlen.

Acknowledgments

Foreword

by William C. Ketchum Jr.

Untitled by Bill Traylor, circa 1940.

Over the past two decades, the number of art and antiques enthusiasts has increased exponentially. Today, millions of Americans create or collect folk art. Writers have been quick to capitalize on this phenomenon, turning out hundreds of books designed to educate the enthusiast. Up to now, however, these texts have been directed solely to the adult market. No one has thought to provide basic information for children and young adults, despite the fact that they represent the next generation.

Richard Panchyk's *American Folk Art for Kids* represents an important first step in the education of these youthful art and antiques lovers, and the field he has chosen is a particularly suitable one. Folk art is readily understood by all. Children who are naturally drawn to painting and sculpture have an affinity for folk expression. After all, it relates directly to life. The child, with enthusiasm and an open mind, can readily accept and appreciate a carved wooden doll or a toy house constructed of Popsicle sticks. Apparent crudeness in construction and failure to follow the accepted canons of academic art, which might turn off a sophisticated adult, will be seen by the youthful enthusiast as signs of playfulness and artistic vigor. In fact, folk art, which springs from the most innate needs and nature of humankind, is the perfect field through which to introduce youth to the world of art and antiques.

Panchyk, moreover, has combined sound introductions to a variety of folk art fields with interesting hands-on projects that allow the reader to experience and explore the same creative feelings that animate the folk artist. This approach draws the child into the crafter's world and supplements the text, making it more readily understandable. In combination, text and projects provide an innovative introduction to folk art that seems guaranteed to produce a new generation of enthusiastic folk art and antique lovers.

We are born with the ability to make art. When a little baby looks at lots of colors, they can relate. Kids start really young. There's something about holding a crayon and doing a swirl. Kids like to make dots and lines. Lots of kids are self-taught from early on. It's almost as if their hands have some type of rhythm, and it's amazing. Lots of kids are actually geniuses. But you can't force it. Art has to be a very natural thing.

Ministry runs in my family. My great-great aunt told me I was going to be a minister. But it turned out I would be a minister of art. I have been working with kids and teenagers and parents for many, many years, and to this day. Parents say, "I can't make art." I tell parents, just try it, just try it. I have taught thousands and thousands and thousands of kids. Lots of kids have told me once they get older they want to be an artist. I run into some of the ones I taught who are adults and have kids of their own. They would say they still have their art pieces they made. Lots of artists have this

wonderful talent but are afraid to share it because someone might steal their ideas. But I am happy if the kids I teach might go back to their neighborhoods and teach others.

First, before doing my workshop, I actually show them what I made, and then I allow them to hold some of my work, like a paintbrush. I let them wear my bottle cap hat, and they remember that. Kids go to a museum and they are not allowed to touch anything. You have to put faith and trust in kids.

I start the workshop by telling kids that I was walking down the street to the store and I heard a sound go like: "Pssst!" Then I heard it again: "Pssst!" I ask, what was that sound. They say, "A cat" or "Someone calling you." Then finally one kid will say, "It was your imagination." I say, "That's right," and that's how I start.

When I give them a piece of sandstone, I would tell them to look into that stone and carve what they see, and if they make a wrong line, they can always

Foreword by Mr. Imagination

erase that and start over. When making art, you cannot make a mistake. A "mistake" can make you see something in another way, and you can grow from that place.

Then I give them glue and art paper so they could use that sand from their carving to do sand paintings by using their imagination. I feel that hands-on is very important for each and every child, but now there are many schools that don't teach art. Art helps them to work together as a team and learn how to solve a problem.

Kids like bottle caps because they have a shine that's magical. I use a wire hanger, modeling clay, and bottle caps to make a snake. One time there was a little girl. I had flattened out a bunch of caps. She got scissors and cut a diamond shape out of the cap. I liked her idea. She actually taught me something.

For many, many years I have been receiving boxes and boxes and boxes of letters from kids, telling me what a wonderful time they had making art. They write and thank me for showing them how to turn trash into treasures. It allowed them to use their imagination. When I'm working with kids and see they're happy, I'm happy too. At the end of each workshop that I have done, everyone leaves with a smile.

When I do workshops with kids, it allows them to not just make art, but it allows them to be able to work together like a team, a skill they will need later in life. I like the fact that the activities in this book can also be done by kids working together.

Folk art is not possible without imagination. I hope that everyone reading this book will open up their mind and explore their own imagination.

An old man goes into his workshop every morning and works until noon making wind toys. He saws and carves wood into cars, trains, and airplanes, then paints and assembles the parts to make these whirligigs, as they are called. For a couple of hours after lunch, he sits at his roadside stand selling these wind toys to passing motorists. To him it is just a fun hobby, a way to pass the time. The old man may not even realize it, but he is a folk artist.

Every Saturday evening, the man puts out a cardboard box of his scraps for the garbage collector to take, but the garbage collector rarely gets a chance to pick them up. Every Sunday morning, a middle-aged woman from down the road rides her bicycle up to the curb. She loads her knapsack with all the scraps. Sometimes the old man sees her and waves. When the woman gets home, she glues the scraps of wood and metal together to make collages. She does not realize it either, but she is also a folk artist.

Folk art is all about taking something ordinary and making it extraordinary. The old man uses some wood and his imagination to make colorful toys. The woman recycles his garbage to make more artworks. If there is one common theme that runs throughout the many different types of folk art that appear in this book, it is that of ordinary people making something out of nothing. From some ordinarily useless scraps of fabric, a woman creates a beautiful quilt. From a plain and simple chair, a folk artist makes a decorated masterpiece. From a shapeless hunk of wood, a duck decoy is carved. A folk artist takes ordinary handwriting and turns it into elegant, flowing calligraphy; takes old fence posts and creates an American flag; takes bottle caps and makes a sculpture.

American folk art developed from the traditions of immigrants coming from all around the world. Folk art celebrates the colorful diversity that is inside each of us, our multicultural heritage passed down over the centuries, and our natural-born ability to create something beautiful. In this book you will read about many different types of folk art that have captured the imagination of millions of people around America and across the globe.

What Is Folk Art?
Introduction

Author's Note

I have tried to organize this book into logical chapters. Because there are so many different types of folk art, it was not an easy task. First I explain the origins of folk art in chapter 1. Then I go into different categories of folk art. There is painting and drawing in chapter 2, decorative designs on furniture and other practical objects, known as the "decorative arts," in chapter 3, textile folk art (made from fabric and yarn) in chapter 4, folk art that is carved from and chiseled into stone, metal, wood, or bone in chapter 5, folk art that is made from scraps of odds and ends, known as "found objects," in chapter 6, and finally, "public" folk art, including advertising, in chapter 7. Though it was impossible to include everything in one book, I have tried to cover all the major types of folk art.

When possible, I have provided exact dates of the art shown in the illustrations, but most folk art is anonymous and undated, so many of the dates given in this book are educated guesses. The word *circa*, which means approximately, is used to indicate that the exact date of a piece of art is not known.

I hope that you enjoy your journey into the world of folk art as much as I have enjoyed writing the book.

The Origins of Folk Art

When the first art was made, there were no museums, no art schools, and no art supply stores. Our early ancestors created small gray stone sculptures using only basic tools. As time passed, art became more colorful and sophisticated. Ice Age people, who lived 15,000 years ago, decorated the walls of their cave homes. Using natural pigments found in berries and stones to "paint" their designs, they created paintings of deer and horses, and they sometimes left behind human handprints.

"U Need Milk 2 Grow" birdhouse,
Jaffrey, New Hampshire, late 20th century.

Art and Civilization

Beginning around 8,000 to 6,000 B.C., many people all around the world gave up their nomadic lives of hunting and gathering. They learned how to domesticate animals and how to grow, cook, and store their own food. People discovered that they could mold clay (a material dug out of the ground) into any shape and bake it at a high temperature to make it hard and durable. Pots, bowls, jars, and other serving and storage items were common. People also began to weave and sew, and they created clothes and blankets.

With the invention of pottery and textiles, humans had another reason to use artistic decoration. Since people no longer changed residences with the seasons, they could have more posses-sions. They decorated their permanent posses-sions, especially items of pottery, with beautiful geometric designs. Many ancient cultures can be identified by the type of design they liked to use. The example shown here is a clay jar from the Majiayao culture of the Chinese Neolithic (New Stone Age) period, which existed over 4,000 years ago. The intricate, often swirly black designs are a characteristic of Majiayao pottery.

As agriculture thrived, tiny villages grew into bustling towns, and towns grew into huge cities of up to 50,000 people. These cities were part of civilizations that had organized forms of govern-ment, controlled large territories, and had very active trade with other parts of the world.

By this time, design and decoration were a key part of the human experience. Archaeologists have found beautifully crafted artworks from all major ancient cultures, including Mesopotamia (the Near East), ancient Egypt, Shang dynasty China, Incan Peru, and ancient Greece and Rome. Each of the different civilizations had its own unique cus-toms, traditions, languages, and artistic designs, and each civilization had people whose only job was to paint, sculpt, or craft jewelry. These people became experts and were known as *artisans*.

But the ancient world did not just consist of a few large civilizations. Thousands of other people

Majiayao Chinese pot, 3000–2000 B.C.

still lived in much smaller bands, or tribes. Each of these tribes also had its own unique traditions and artwork. Some groups were warriors or nomads in search of new territory. These tribes helped destroy the Roman Empire in the 5th century A.D. After the Empire crumbled, the "barbarian" tribes (a Roman term for "uncivilized" people) moved in to control various parts of Europe.

Until about 1000 A.D., roving bands of people continued to migrate from the northern and eastern reaches of Europe and from western and central Asia in search of better land. Some tribal names are familiar, while others have long since faded into obscurity: Pechenegs, Cumans, Angles, Saxons, Gauls, Kimaks, Ghuzz, Khazars, Jutes, Celts, Magyars, Visigoths, Franks, Burgundii, Vikings, Turks, Bulgars, and Normans.

Descendants of many of these ancient ethnic groups still exist. The old Normans are gone, but many English people are of Norman descent. Similarly, Hungary has many Magyar descendants, and many Turkish people are descendants of the Turks.

But even countries that seem to be truly one distinct culture today—Germany, for example—are not really one culture. The people in different parts of Germany are descended from different tribes, so people living in Bavaria (in southern Germany) are different from people living in Thuringia (in central Germany), for example. The differences in their art, food, and music appear slight to the outsider, but they are very clear to the people who live there.

Folk Art Emerges

The number of artisans and craftspeople, who emerged when the first civilizations were created, continued to grow. They were an important part of every town or city, and they had access to the finest materials and tools. By the 13th and 14th centuries, many had begun to form *guilds*. These guilds were groups that set rules and quality guidelines for a particular craft. The most experienced artists were known as masters, and their assistants and students were called apprentices. Also emerging around this time were talented professional painters who were commissioned to create religious works for churches and portraits for wealthy individuals.

In addition to the trained artists who created art for a living, there were many people who were not professional artists but who also painted and decorated. They did not always have access to the finest materials or tools, but that did not discourage them. Some painted designs on their furniture. Others decorated plain pottery vessels. Some were traveling artists who did not belong to any guild but went from place to place looking for customers. The colorful folk traditions of the "barbarian" tribes continued to be practiced by amateur artists in villages across Europe long after the tribes fell apart. These amateur painters, carvers, and traveling artists were the first true folk artists.

Early folk art designs are still used today. Though many of today's folk art items are mass-produced in factories with scarcely a human hand touching them in the process, their designs date back to art created hundreds or thousands of years ago. Common everyday modern items such as sweaters, wallpaper, and playing cards often feature elaborate colorful designs with long histories attached to them.

The Geography of Folk Art

Folk artists from the same ethnic group do not always create the same type of art. It depends on their environment—what their living conditions are like. For example, take three Ukrainian folk artists. Place one of them in a village by the sea, drop another in a village high up in the mountains, and leave the third in a village deep in the forest. Each one will still be a Ukrainian with Ukrainian traditions and culture, but each will develop new twists on his or her culture as the art is created.

The Ukrainian by the sea might make pictures of ships and make models of fish, use shells to make a mosaic, use coral to make a sculpture, and make a box laden with mother-of-pearl. The Ukrainian in the mountains may paint snowy scenes and make carvings of goats and other mountain animals. Since trees may be hard to find in the mountains, so that artist may make carvings from stone. The Ukrainian in the forest, where there are many trees, might carve walking sticks out of wood, collect leaves and flowers to make a collage, and incorporate bears, deer, rabbits, and other forest animals in his or her artwork.

Similarly, a folk artist who lives in a city will make different artworks than a folk artist who lives

Kalocsa embroidered tablecloth, circa 1970.

in the country or in a suburb. One village may have very different folk traditions from the next one just a few miles away. Village X may lie near a huge field of flowers, while Village Y might stand next to a roaring river. Over time, the inhabitants of each village develop their own unique art. For

Watercolor of a rose, late 19th century.

example, the inhabitants of Kalocsa, Hungary, developed a unique flowery folk art that is not found anywhere else in the world.

Folk artists are influenced by three key things: their own natural talents, the culture they grew up with, and the climate and geography of the places in which they live. This is an important thing to remember when studying folk art in this book. When you look at a piece of folk art, try to guess how the artist's background and location might have affected the art.

American Folk Art

The first true American folk art was created by Native Americans. Migrating from Asia thousands of years ago, hundreds of tribes spread throughout North and South America. Over time, each tribe developed its own artistic traditions. Using animal skins, wood, stone, and natural dyes, Native Americans created colorful masterpieces.

During the early 17th century, Native Americans were joined by the first European settlers, who came at first by the hundreds and later by the thousands and then millions. These immigrants, who came to the United States from hundreds of countries, brought some of their own cultural heritages with them. Waves of people came to the United States because of famine, poverty, and oppression in their homeland. A search for religious freedom brought many 17th-century English immigrants. The Potato Famine of 1848 caused a huge number of Irish people to emigrate. Poverty and hard times in Germany caused large numbers

of Germans to sail to the United States during the late 19th century. By the 20th century, immigrants were also streaming in from Asia, Africa, and South and Central America.

Immigrants to the United States tended to settle in different places depending on their country of origin. They spread across the United States in every direction. Many of today's Midwesterners are descended from Scandinavians; Pennsylvanians and Ohioans from Germans; Louisianans from Acadians (from Canada); and New Englanders from English and Irish. Slavery brought many Africans to the southern United States, and the building of the transcontinental railroad brought many Chinese to California.

The Europeans pushed the Native Americans off their land and introduced diseases that killed a great many of them. By the late 19th century, the crush of newcomers to America was so great that the Native Americans were forced onto "reservations," land set aside just for their use. Their cultures still thrived into the 20th century, however, and Native Americans around the country continue to create artworks both for their own use and for tourists.

The new European, African, and Asian arrivals created art in the style of their home countries, and it is this rainbow of immigrant cultures from around the world that gives American folk art its colorful flavor. American folk art has a beautifully mixed heritage that reflects the diversity of the American population.

Though it had existed since the 17th century, American folk art was not truly appreciated until

Watercolor of father and child, early 19th century.

1924, when the first major folk art exhibit in the country was put together in New York City. Called Early American Art, the exhibit at the Whitney Studio Club featured 45 works of folk art. The timing was right for the exhibit because in the 1920s, people were nostalgic for their past. Civil War (1861–1865) veterans were beginning to die off rapidly, and there were revivals of interest in the Civil War era, as well as in the Colonial and Federal periods (17th to early 19th century). Other museums followed with groundbreaking folk art exhibits during the 1930s. At that point, many masterpieces of American folk art were gathering dust in attics and basements, were part of private collections, or were hanging on the walls of local historical societies in towns across America. During the 1930s, President Franklin Roosevelt's WPA (Works Progress Administration) program cataloged many of the finest pieces of folk art in the country. As the generation that grew up during the Victorian era (middle to late 19th century) grew old during the early and middle 20th century, there was a revival of interest in the art of that time period.

At first, only certain types of artwork, such as folk painting created before 1900, were considered to be folk art. As time passed, though, more and more categories of American arts and crafts were recognized as folk art. A talented woman named Grandma Moses created beautiful nostalgic paintings during the 1940s and 1950s that appealed to millions of Americans. She was the first true living folk art celebrity. Her popularity made it possible for other folk artists to get recognition during their lifetimes.

In 1957, the wealthy Mrs. John D. Rockefeller's large folk art collection found a permanent home in a building in Colonial Williamsburg, Virginia. By 1961, there was enough interest in folk art that the American Folk Art Museum was established. During the 1960s, the United States Postal Service began to issue stamps celebrating folk art. Around this time, more and more people began to realize that 20th-century folk art could be just as wonderful as 19th-century folk art.

By the 1980s, numerous books about folk art were written, auctions of folk art treasures became a regular happening, and new folk art museums sprang up across the country. Suddenly, pieces of art that had sold for just a few dollars 50 years before were worth thousands of dollars. Today, American folk art keeps growing in popularity. In 2001, the American Folk Art Museum in New York City moved from cramped quarters to a spacious new seven-story building, allowing a much larger stream of visitors to see folk art treasures or do research among the 10,000 books in its collection.

American folk art today boasts a rich diversity and history that few other countries can rival. It is a fun field where new folk art masterpieces are still being created every day in every corner of the country, and where exciting antique finds still turn up. Folk art in America shows just how inventive, creative, and talented ordinary people can be. It shows how Americans recycle scraps of their precious resources such as wood and fabric. Folk art is all about taking advantage of spare time by creating something beautiful.

American folk art is definitely not stuck in the past. It is still going strong today, and it shows no sign of slowing down. The following chapters offer examples of recently created folk art as well as examples of older folk art.

Activity

Find Your Folk Roots

The first Europeans, Asians, and Africans who entered the Americas within the last 400 years brought their folk traditions with them, while Native Americans have been creating folk art here for thousands of years. In this activity, you will trace your own cultural roots and see what kinds of folk traditions your ancestors had.

MATERIALS

Notebook (8½ by 11 inches)

Pencil

Map of the world

Camera

Tourist brochures or photos

All-purpose glue

Ask your parents or grandparents to sketch out your family tree in your notebook for you. Where did your ancestors come from? Make a list of the different countries that come up in the family tree and mark them on a map. Ask your parents, aunts, uncles, grandparents, and cousins if they have any "traditional" clothes, paintings, decorations, or knickknacks that you can photograph. Some items you might find are: decorative ornaments, drawings, paintings, dolls, clothes, tablecloths, rugs, ceramics (plates, vases, statuettes), and painted furniture. Gather some information about your ancestral countries. Look up the countries' tourist offices on the Internet or write to the tourist boards or consulates and ask them to send you brochures. Print or clip out any colorful pictures that show some of the folk costumes, folk art, or culture of the place your ancestors were from. You can also go to the library and make photocopies of any pictures you find. Glue your pictures into the notebook to make a scrapbook all about your folk ancestry.

Folk Painting and Drawing

Paintings do much more than capture a fleeting moment. They express our deepest emotions and our wildest imagination, our dearest hopes and our darkest fears. Paintings are powerful objects that can freeze the image of a beloved family member or friend, a quiet day in a farm village, a colorful sunset, or a ship sailing amid a violent storm at sea. Paintings are also decorative items that can brighten up a room and provide enjoyment. People living in big cities may enjoy paintings of the countryside to remind them of the greenery that is missing from their environment.

People who love the sea may fill their homes with paintings of ships and lighthouses, while animal lovers may own wildlife paintings. A wealthy person can buy an expensive painting or commission one (pay for someone to paint exactly what she wants), but it isn't necessary to be rich to own art. Anybody can enjoy owning a painting, whether it's one that's inexpensive to buy or one painted by the owner himself or herself.

Academic Painting and Folk Painting

Throughout recent history, professional artists were often specially trained to paint in certain ways. They learned the popular styles of the day, and their work was accepted by both the art world and their paying customers. To learn their craft, they studied under masters. When they became skilled, they often taught their own students, or apprentices.

This tradition is called academic painting. Not only did academic painters study with trained artists, but they were also part of the local art community. They made friends with other academic painters, were commissioned by rich and famous people to paint, and showed their works at galleries and exhibitions.

Most folk paintings, on the other hand, were done by people who had little or no formal artistic training. They may not have known or cared about the "acceptable" painting styles of the time. These people may not have made a living by making art

and probably did not know other artists. The lives of academic painters are well documented in art books, but the lives of most folk painters are not documented. Even today, many folk painters work anonymously, meaning that they do not sign their paintings. Folk paintings are artworks by "common people."

There are different names for various kinds of folk paintings and drawings. Most folk paintings can be classified under one or more of the categories described below.

Outsider art is any art that is made outside the regular process that academic artists follow, such as attending art school, showing their work at galleries, and having contact with many other artists. The reclusive old man who paints every day in his tiny dark apartment but only shows his artwork to a few friends and family members is an outsider artist. The reclusive old man who paints every day in his tiny dark apartment but who has many artist friends and an agent to represent him, and who sells his work through a gallery, is not an outsider artist.

An outsider may or may not have had some artistic training, but he or she produces art outside the academic art world. Many outsiders die before their work is ever discovered and shown in public. Often, outsiders live in rural areas and have limited exposure to the world of art. One exception is the now-famous and controversial outsider artist Henry Darger (1892–1973), who lived in a cluttered apartment in the large city of Chicago, and

Scene from a greeting card, mid-20th century.

created bizarre and sometimes disturbing images featuring children to illustrate his fantasy stories.

Art collectors have recently taken a strong interest in outsider art. There are outsider art fairs held in prestigious places, and many outsider artists' works can now be found for sale on the Internet or in galleries. It is hard to say if these artists are still "outsiders" now that they are receiving so much exposure and attention. Take the case of John Mason, whose pencil and crayon drawings, done after he reached the age of 90, sell for prices starting at $100 each.

Patients at Creedmoor Psychiatric Center in Queens, New York, are given the chance to express their artistic sides in a special studio and museum that was created on the premises. Some of these artists have gone on to become known figures in the world of outsider art.

Self-taught is a term that applies to anyone who creates art but who has not had formal training. This does not mean that a self-taught artist must live in a cave with no exposure to others' art. In this modern world, almost everyone has access to television, computers, and books, so even a self-taught artist can easily see examples of what Rembrandt, Claude Monet, Jasper Johns, and hundreds of other artists have painted. The difference is that these people paint or create art their own way, with little interest in making it correct or acceptable to the art world. They do not follow the rules of academic painting. Instead, they use only their own instincts. While they may have access to the great art of the past, they do not have training to duplicate the brush strokes and effects they see.

Everything they create is based purely on their own natural talents.

Self-taught artists often begin their careers when they are older, after they retire from jobs that do not involve art. Bill Traylor (1856–1949) was a former slave who could not read or write and who did not start drawing until he was 83. Then, in the space of three years, he created more than 1,500 works of art while sitting on a sidewalk in Alabama. Another man, Harry Lieberman (1880–1983), took up painting in his mid-70s and continued until he died at the age of 103.

What about someone who has shown interest in art and has made an effort to learn more by taking classes? They are no longer self-taught, but may still be an outsider. On the other hand, some self-taught artists, such as Howard Finster (see page 33), become so popular and accepted during their lifetimes, it is questionable if they are still outsiders.

Visionary art is a term that usually applies to art that is created from a dream or vision that the artist has had. Sometimes it is a onetime dream that makes a deep impression. Other times it is a recurring dream or vision that shapes the person's everyday life. Annie Wellborn of Georgia (1928–), says that she is visited by angels whom she believes are departed relatives. She often depicts these angels in her paintings. She also paints the balls of fire that she "sees" before someone she knows dies. She began to paint at about age 60, after having a vision in which she was told she should paint. Many visionary artists have a near-death experience and are suddenly consumed with the passion to make art afterward.

Watermelons by Annie Wellborn, date unknown.

Untitled #4 by Peter Prommersberger, 1965.

Primitive art is defined as unrefined or naive art that has childlike qualities. An outsider painting may or may not be primitive, depending on its appearance. When a painting or drawing is simple in style and coloring, the word *primitive* is often used. Still, not just any old scribbling on paper is a primitive artwork. Primitive art is enjoyed because it has a certain charm and friendliness that draws the viewer inside. It is unique and has character. A great piece of primitive art is never as simple as it looks. It is rich, colorful, and filled with many visual treats. A primitive artist may or may not also be an outsider or a self-taught artist.

The landscape painting seen here was done in crisp colors and careful detail by a self-taught outsider. It was among his first attempts at art, a hobby that he has continued for over 35 years. What do you think it is about this painting that qualifies it as primitive?

Primitive art is very popular today, and artists deliberately paint in that style to create quaint pictures they can sell. Other artists paint that way because it is the only way to paint that they know. Other words used to describe primitive art are "rustic" and "country." Some primitive paintings are known as "shabby chic" in fancy galleries and shops.

Art brut, or "raw art," is a term applied to a specific type of art that is made mostly by outsiders. These paintings are not naive or rustic like a primitive work, but are jarring and bold. Art brut works appear emotionally charged and intense. While other folk art may have emotional undertones, art brut brings pure, raw emotion right to the surface. Some other words that could be applied to art brut might be: wild, imaginative, surreal, scary, violent, instinctive, jagged, and powerful. An art brut painting could be a depiction of a bad dream or an unpleasant memory, for example.

Folk Portraits

Have you ever had your picture taken by a professional photographer? You sat still for a couple of seconds, and then for a few dollars you got

Drawing of Joseph Henry Collier, late 1850s.

some glossy photos of yourself—an exact duplication of your face, down to every last detail. But 200 years ago, there was no such thing as a camera. All portraits were paintings, and you had to sit for a lot longer than a few seconds, so that the painter could capture the details of your face—the thickness of your lips, the shape of your nose, and the exact color of your eyes. Well-known academic painters such as Charles Willson Peale (1741–1827) were commissioned to paint portraits of wealthy and famous people, including George Washington. Average Americans who wanted portraits painted hired "limners" (from the French word *luminer*, meaning to illuminate or make clear), traveling folk painters who plied their trade over an area of a few hundred miles. These folk paintings were not as finely painted as academic portraits, but they had a certain warmth that people really admired. Though limners were not necessarily artistically trained, they had a knack for capturing the essence of a person in a few quick brush strokes.

New England painter William Matthew Prior (1806–1873) is the best-known folk portrait painter of the 19th century. He worked in the same style as his wife's painter relatives, the Hamblins. Their style of portrait painting became known as the Prior-Hamblin School. Today, Prior's paintings bring top dollar at auction, but there are many anonymous works that are just as fine as Prior's. For his bargain price, Prior promised solid work, but with no "shade or shadows," meaning that the portrait would look very flat and two-dimensional. At the cut-rate prices they charged, limners could not afford to spend too long on their paint-

ings, so the sacrifice of shading and dimension helped shave off some time. The speed at which Prior painted is evident in the example of the young girl shown here. His talent was to capture the basic likeness of people quickly and effectively, leaving behind satisfied customers who would recommend him to others.

Painting of a girl with flowers, attributed to William Matthew Prior, 1830–1850.

The Hobby of Folk Art

A few folk artists become well known and are able to support themselves by selling their work. Some, like Grandma Moses and, to a lesser extent, Howard Finster, are "discovered" and become nationally famous, and their popularity continues after their deaths.

The rest of the nation's folk artists practice their craft as a hobby, something they do on the side. Many folk artists are retired from their jobs, giving them the free time to spend as they please. Others pursue their love of creating during evenings and weekends. Some make and sell folk art on the Internet, in gift shops, or at roadside stands. Although some hope to one day be able to live off their art, the main reason folk artists create art is because they love what they are doing. Any money they make from selling their artworks is usually seen as icing on the cake.

Some of the best-loved and most valuable folk portraits show children. Clutching toys, the children are never smiling—it was not considered proper to smile for paintings or photographs until the 20th century. The girls and boys depicted are usually elegantly dressed, with the girls in long red or blue velvet dresses and the boys in crisp-looking suits. After all, the painting of a portrait was a special occasion; it might be years later, if ever, that a person ever had his or her portrait painted again. The drawing on page 14 dates to the late 1850s, and shows bright-eyed and dapper young Joseph Henry Collier (born 1845) all dressed up, complete with a walking stick. The son of Joseph and Rebecca Collier, Joseph Henry was one of six children in the middle-class Collier family, who lived near Harrisburg, Pennsylvania. Whether it was a family member or a professional limner who drew him we may never know, but it was obviously someone with an artistic eye.

One of the most important folk portrait paintings is the famous *Girl in Red Dress with Cat and Dog* by Ammi Phillips (1788–1865), painted in upstate New York. Against a dark background, a little girl in an expensive bright red dress sits holding a white cat, while a dog lies sleepily at her feet. Phillips, whose paintings are treasured today, was very detail oriented. He tried to provide exact replication of the sitter, down to the finer details of the clothing he or she wore.

Some excellent folk painters did not sign their works. An artist known only as the Beardsley Limner (after the names of two of his subjects, Mr. and Mrs. Hezekiah Beardsley) painted at least 20 portraits in New England during the late 18th and early 19th centuries. Another portrait painter is known as the Freake-Gibbs Painter, after two families he likely painted in Boston.

Folk portraits were painted on canvas and on paper, and they were also done on ivory or porcelain in a miniature format that could be kept in a locket, in the pocket, or perhaps on a hutch shelf. In keeping with German tradition, the Pennsylvania Dutch and other German immigrants painted folk portraits of brides and grooms onto wooden bride's boxes, a gift for the bride that would be used to store some of the couple's valuable possessions.

Folk painting was very popular for many years. Then, in the late 1830s, a Frenchman named Louis Jacques Mande Daguerre went public with his new invention—a process to capture an image on a plate of copper coated with silver. The first "daguerreotypes," as they were called, were not nearly as crisp as modern photographs, but nevertheless, portrait painting would never be the same. By the 1840s, important people, including former presidents John Quincy Adams and Andrew Jackson, and painter/inventor Samuel F. B. Morse, chose to have photographers rather than painters do their portraits. But the advantage of painters was their ability to create large, colorful portraits, while the camera could only produce small black-and-white portraits. Painters' affordable prices, which ranged from two to three dollars at the time, kept some portrait painters in business for a while, but by the mid-1860s, professional folk portrait painting had almost died out.

American Railroads by Robert C. Shanahan, 1942.

information about the artist's environment. Like a snapshot in time, a folk art landscape painting or drawing shows many things going on at once—a whole miniature world of people and emotions and events. Folk paintings may not be realistic, like a photograph, but they are always colorful and interesting.

As in the *American Railroads* piece shown here, every little detail is done with great care. A person could look at the artwork for an hour and keep finding new details. In the railroad master-piece, the artist has re-created a scene from a late 19th century industrial town, probably in western New York or Ohio. The vibrant pastel colors are almost surreal; a fantasy of what life was like in the "good old days." Perhaps the artist, Robert Shanahan, was remembering his childhood days. Perhaps he was born in 1867, and that is why he wrote his name and the year 1867 on the coach car. On the other hand, perhaps he was a young man just imagining what life might have been like in the 1800s. Either way, he created a cheerful picture that makes us wish we were there. The judges of a contest the picture was entered in must have thought the same thing, because a paper attached to the back of the painting says "Robert C. Shanahan, 2nd and 3rd Prizes."

Even though most professional folk portrait painting stopped before the late 19th century, amateurs to this day continue to paint portraits for their own personal enjoyment. Some of these folk paintings have as much primitive charm as their old-time cousins.

Landscape Paintings

Folk art portraits are windows into the minds and hearts of people from many different places and times. When an artist chooses to show us a scene of a street or village or city, we get even more

Landscape paintings often show scenes of the area where the art was painted. Busy streets, heavy industry, and the progress of technology were the focus of paintings created in cities. Peaceful rolling hills, fall foliage, and winter scenes were characteristic of the Northeastern paintings. The folk painting of Texas shown on page 19 shows the dry

Activity

Paint a Folk Portrait

Painting a folk portrait requires no special training. All you need are some basic materials and a person who is willing to sit for you (it can be a friend, a teacher, or a relative). You might want to give your subject something to hold while he or she poses. In old folk portraits, the subjects can be seen holding books, toys, sewing baskets, quill pens, flowers, and pets.

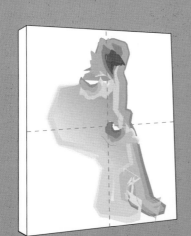

MATERIALS

- Canvas or canvas board (at least 9 by 12 inches)
- Willing subject
- Pencil
- Acrylic paints (white, black, brown, yellow, red, green, blue, and any other colors you like)
- Palette (available at an art or crafts store) or a Styrofoam plate
- Palette knife
- Paint brushes of different sizes

Lean the canvas up against a chair. Ask your subject to sit in a comfortable chair and take the pose you want to paint. Don't be intimidated. Painting someone's likeness is not that hard, if you break it down into some basic questions. First, what shape is his or her head? How far down are the eyes from the top of the head? A third of the way? About halfway down? How big is the nose? How wide is the mouth and how thick are the lips? Using the pencil, try to sketch the general head shape and key features of your subject. It may help to divide your canvas into a grid of four rectangles to make the sketching easier and more symmetrical. Now you are ready to paint your sketch. Squirt a little of each color of paint onto your palette, about an inch apart. Use the palette knife to mix some white paint with red, yellow, and brown until you get the right color for your subject's skin. When your color is right, use paintbrushes to paint your portrait. Remember that the keys to painting a portrait are putting your subject's features in the right places and getting the proportions correct. Sign and date your painting so future folk art scholars will know something about your work.

Name that Painting

Unlike their academic counterparts, many folk art paintings are not signed and do not have a title. Signatures and titles are more of an academic tradition, where a painter's name is important to the buyer and the title is engraved on a brass plaque on the frame. The title is there so that the artist and his clients can refer to the particular painting by name. The amateur who is painting at home may not feel the need to title or sign a painting. What names would you give to the untitled paintings in this chapter?

Woman with two children,
painted on porcelain,
mid- to late 19th century.

climate and some unique features of the Southwest, including an armadillo, Spanish moss hanging from the tree, a cactus, and a bunch of peppers hanging out to dry. Scenes of life also vary with the era in which they were painted. For example, in 19th-century paintings you might see horse-drawn carriages, and in 20th-century paintings you might see automobiles.

Some folk landscape paintings are painted as if the scene is viewed from the air. Known as "bird's-eye views," these paintings were often done to show the impressive growth of towns or cities. Views of factories show the offices, storerooms, stables, and factory buildings of the large complexes that were a product of the Industrial Revolution.

While portrait painting decreased after the 19th century, landscape painting continues to be popular to this day. Modern (post-1945) folk landscapes depict modern life in the same charming way that "old-time" paintings capture peaceful days on the farm or in the village. Though Norman Rockwell's paintings of American life during the 1950s and 1960s capture funny and interesting moments that have a folklike quality, Rockwell was

Paintings of suburban life by Margaret Leyden Wagner, circa 1940s.

What Makes It a Good Painting?

Painting of Texas landscape by Dutz, 1928.

Painting of a camp scene, early 20th century.

Painted in a primitive style, this early-20th-century camp scene shows three faceless figures gathered around a red, smoldering campfire, with tents and an American flag in the background. Two figures are seated and the third is standing in an odd pose. The trees, clouds, and hills are all painted very simply. Except for the flag and sky, the colors are neutral earth tones.

There are thousands of primitive landscape paintings out there, and many of them are just average—not exceptionally good, valuable, or interesting. When is a folk painting something special? A good one contains details that draw the viewer into the picture; strange and fascinating little touches that transform the painting from ordinary to extraordinary. An academic painting is judged by its pleasing or beautiful touches, but with folk art it is the odd, the out of the ordinary, and the quirky that can separate average from superb. Some of the details that make this camp scene interesting are the dancing figure, the little "s" of smoke rising from the fire, the open tent flap, the brightly painted flag, and the fact that the figures have no faces.

not a folk artist, but a commercial artist who painted for magazine covers.

The paintings by Margaret Leyden Wagner (1915–2000) shown on page 18 was likely done during the late 1940s. It appears to have been carefully copied from a photo or advertisement in a monthly home or garden magazine. It helps to know a little bit about the artist to understand the reason she painted scenes such as this. Wagner grew up in a large city, and then moved to the suburbs during the early 1930s. She and her father enjoyed gardening very much; he won medals for his gardens. An enthusiastic artist, she painted whenever she got the chance. She had a talent for taking a fake (staged) scene that was used in a magazine and giving it a life of its own in her painting. Just as Grandma Moses celebrated the joys of country life on the farm, Wagner celebrated her joys—gardening and

The most famous and best-loved folk painter of the 20th century was Grandma Moses. Unlike many famous folk artists, Grandma Moses became a legend while she was still alive. Born Anna Mary Robertson on a farm in upstate New York, she married Thomas Moses, gave birth to 10 children, and had a peaceful life before being thrust into stardom at the age of 80. She had only begun painting, when she was a widow in her 70s, because her arthritis made it difficult to do the needlework she enjoyed. The life she led was very rustic. The town where she lived—Eagle Bridge, New York—was the perfect setting to inspire landscape paintings that featured beautiful scenery and tranquil rural village life. Her home did not even have plumbing until the 1930s.

In 1938, her work was accidentally discovered by a collector named Louis Caldor, who happened to see several of her paintings displayed in the window of the town drugstore. He bought several of her paintings and launched her career by bringing her to the attention of a gallery owner in New York City named Otto Kallir.

Grandma Moses had her first solo art show in 1940, at Kallir's Galerie St. Etienne in New York City. The show was called "What a Farm Wife Painted." Grandma Moses's charming landscape paintings were primitive and colorful. Her arrival on the art scene happened just as the world was entering World War II, and Americans longed to remember the simpler and more peaceful past. Grandma Moses's natural

Sugaring Off by Grandma Moses, 1943.

talent and charm, combined with good timing, made her very successful.

Hildegard Bachert, whose family had fled Nazi Germany a few years before, was employed at the gallery when Grandma Moses arrived on the scene. They first met on one of Moses's rare trips to New York City. The occasion was a display of her work at Gimbel's Department Store's Thanksgiving festival in November 1940. Bachert was amazed at all the commotion

surrounding the frail-looking little old lady who was the center of attention. Bachert developed a close friendship with Grandma Moses, beginning with a train trip to her old house in Eagle Bridge in 1942. On that first trip, Bachert got a tour of the house, met Grandma's son and daughter-in-law who lived with her, and had a look at the artist's work as the two got acquainted. "That was a very, very wonderful meeting," Bachert recalls.

Over the years they grew very close, and Bachert visited Grandma Moses about five times a year. "I got to know every corner of that house," says Bachert. Because the Galerie St. Etienne was the exclusive representative of Grandma Moses, Bachert got to spend a lot of time with her and even observe her at work. She brought an 8-mm movie camera one day and filmed Moses while she painted, but the camera did not bother her. "She just went along and did what she had to do." In fact, nothing seemed to bother her. "She was at ease, up to any situation," says Bachert. Grandma Moses became like a grandmother to Bachert, who learned a lot about farming and life in the country while visiting Eagle Bridge. Those trips helped Bachert understand Moses and her artwork. Moses always asked Bachert about her family and friends in New York. She took a real interest in people's lives.

Bachert watched as Grandma Moses's fame grew. In 1946, her paintings were put on millions of greeting cards. She was invited to Washington to meet President Harry S Truman, and in 1955 she was interviewed for CBS television by the most important reporter of the time, Edward R. Murrow. Bachert helped edit Grandma Moses's autobiography and even took dictation when Moses grew tired of writing. It was difficult to keep up, but luckily Bachert knew some shorthand. All the while, Grandma Moses kept things in perspective and retained her sense of humor. The press loved her, but "when reporters asked her silly questions, she gave them ridiculous answers," says Bachert.

"She was totally modest about her success," Bachert remembers. "She never changed her way of life, she didn't spend more on herself. She stayed the same because she had that strength of character." Grandma Moses was at ease with her fame, and was never pompous or fazed by success, according to Bachert.

By the time of her death at the age of 101, Grandma Moses was a world-famous artist whose paintings were bought by collectors and whose scenes appeared on countless millions of Christmas cards. She had even been featured in *Time* and *Life* magazines. Though she started late in life, Grandma Moses completed over 1,500 works of art before her death. "Only after her death did we really learn how she painted," says Bachert. In the early 1980s, the Galerie St. Etienne purchased the preliminary sketches and source material that Moses used for her work. The Galerie St. Etienne runs Grandma Moses Properties, which oversees the use of Grandma Moses's art in books, television, and commercial products. More than half a century after their first meeting, Hildegard Bachert is still hard at work maintaining the legacy of the woman who was a dear friend to her.

Grandma Moses's story shows that often a big part of folk art's appeal is its depiction of how life was when things were "simpler." As time passes, we value these images of the past more and more, as if they are our only connection to those times.

the simple pleasures of suburban life. Leyden did a few other similar paintings, all showing a pleasant suburban house and a woman enjoying her yard.

Watercolor, Pastel, and Tempera Paintings

Watercolors were the most popular type of paint during the 19th century. They are very versatile because the colors can be made lighter or darker depending on how much water is added to the paint. After painting with watercolors, brushes can be cleaned with just water, unlike those that are used for painting with oil-based paint, which requires turpentine. In addition, they do not smell bad, like oil paints do. This has made watercolors popular with children and adults alike for centuries.

Common 19th-century watercolor subjects were birds, flowers, houses, and landscapes. Watercolor pictures have a softness to them that was very appealing to Victorian tastes. Paper is the best medium on which to paint watercolors, so it is a relatively inexpensive hobby for the aspiring artist. Watercolor painting was also considered a "proper" hobby for a Victorian era girl or woman to practice. Painters who specialize in watercolors are known as "watercolorists."

Pastels are made from chalk, pigment, and a mixture called gum water and formed into sticks. They come in dozens of colors, including the pale, cheery ones that we call pastel colors (hence the name). Like watercolors, they are easy to use. An art salesman wrote this to an acquaintance who purchased a set of 40 pastels in 1946:

Watercolor painting of a color grid and a tropical bird
by Harriet Kittle, mid-19th century.

Because of their chalky nature, pastels can smudge easily, so a "fixative" has to be applied that protects the colors and makes them permanent. Like water-colors, pastels work very well on paper. Several 19th-century impressionist artists, including Manet and Degas, liked using pastels.

Tempera paints are made primarily of eggs and pigment, a formula used for over a thousand years. Have you ever seen cookies or bread with a glossy coating on top? Chances are they were coated with an "egg wash," a brushed-on glaze made from eggs. Egg whites in particular are excellent sealers, and they form a very tough and resistant film.

Maritime Folk Art

What is it about ships in water that is so fascinating to artists? Is it the sight of choppy green-blue seas and their white frothy wave caps meeting crisp blue or stormy dark gray skies? Is it the sense of motion and adventure that these images convey? Is it the freedom of the vast ocean? Because the sea is ever changing, it is certainly a more challenging subject to capture than an ordinary landscape.

It might be a combination of all these things that has made paintings of the sea (also known as seascapes, or maritime paintings) so popular over the centuries. Remember that life anywhere along the coast of the United States used to be completely dependent upon ships. Before the age of trucks and airplanes, people often traveled by ship, and goods were commonly shipped from one place to another. Ships played a very important role in history, and many artists, including folk artists,

Painting of a battleship, probably the USS *Kearsarge*, by F. A. Smith, 1902.

Here are the pastels for your niece. I hope she will like them. There are several graded colors, and being that she is so interested in color painting, she will find these very convenient to her finger-tips. In other words, she has no mixing to do. It is all at hand. She will learn to love the touch of pastels. No odor. No preparation. Always handy and the colors at a moment's notice. When inspiration comes, dash for the pastels.

What is needed? Just the colors. A few thumb-tacks. A sheet of paper and a drawing board. Presto! A picture!

Mystery Solved

Many maritime paintings were anonymously painted or are of unnamed or imaginary ships. Once in a rare while, though, there are enough clues in the picture to help viewers figure out what ship is shown. The painting shown here is signed "F. A. Smith" and is dated 1902. It was obtained from a dealer in New Jersey. It shows a United States battleship sailing at full steam in somewhat dark gray-blue seas. Eight sailors are depicted on the deck of the mustard-and-white colored ship. Two guns are mounted on turrets at both the aft (front) and stern (back) of the ship.

The back of the painting has a label that reads "F. W. Devoe & Co. Academy Board [a type of high-quality cardboard used to paint on] corner of Fulton and William Sts., New York." A check of U.S. battleship history shows that there were only 10 battleships in existence in the year 1902, and only one class, or type, of battleship resembled the one in this picture. Of the *Kearsarge* class ships, only the USS *Kearsarge* was in the United States in 1902. In fact, it was the flagship of the Atlantic Coast, and it toured along the coast around that time. Mystery solved!

created beautiful paintings of them throughout the years.

The best maritime paintings capture a moment of life at sea. They feature interesting details and an overall sense of color and motion that draw viewers into the picture. The great Danish-born painter Antonio Jacobsen (1850–1921) loved ships. He came to New York City in the 1870s, where he wound up painting instead of becoming a musician as his father had hoped. Jacobsen loved ships so much that he devoted his life to painting them— everything from tugboats to sailing ships, although steamships were his favorite. During his lifetime, he completed well over 2,000 maritime paintings, each one richly colored and accurately detailed.

Ships remain a popular subject today, and ship paintings are still produced all over the world. Many of these are quickly done renderings of old-time ships that do not exist anymore. The Maine-born artist Earl Cunningham (1893–1977) painted primitive seascapes with old-fashioned ships and modern, vivid colors such as bright blues, crisp yellows, and deep oranges. The best paintings are usually those created from real-life observation. Some of the finest maritime paintings show unique ships such as the battleship seen here. Many people painted rowboats and sailboats, but very few painted battleships, partly because few people ever saw a battleship in person.

Religious Painting

The best-known religious folk painter is Edward Hicks (1780–1849), a Quaker minister who lived in Pennsylvania. So obsessed was Hicks with the Bible that he painted almost a hundred versions of the same painting—*The Peaceable Kingdom*, based on a verse by Isaiah in the Old Testament.

This verse represents the prophet Isaiah's vision for what will happen when all creatures can live together in peace:

> The wolf also shall lay down with the lamb, and the leopard shall lie down with the kid; and the calf and the young lion and the fatling [an animal being fattened for slaughter] together; and a little child shall lead them. And the cow and bear shall feed; their young ones shall lie down together; and the lion shall eat straw like the ox. And the suckling [breastfeeding] child shall play of the asp [a type of snake], and the weaned child shall put his hand on the cockatrice's [a type of snake] den.

Hicks painted all these animals and children exactly as described, and in the background he painted Pennsylvania's founder William Penn purchasing land from the Native Americans. Penn was a Quaker who wanted to create a colony where religious and political freedom were offered to settlers. He was unique among colonist leaders in his friendly relations with the Indians. The paintings were Hicks's religious comment about how Penn was in a way fulfilling the ancient prophecy of Isaiah. In Hicks's paintings it seems as if the child is leading the animals toward Penn, and into the land of Pennsylvania.

Different folk artists focused on different aspects of the Bible. Shaker artists were known to paint the Tree of Life, the biblical tree that the Lord planted in the Garden of Eden, as described in the opening pages of Genesis. The minister William Blayney (1917–1986) used his paintings to emphasize the subjects of his sermons, and he included in his paintings biblical quotes and scenes from many different parts of the Bible.

One reason the Bible was such a common source for ideas was the nearly endless number of possibilities it offered; for every page of the Bible, at least four different scenes could be painted. Other common religious subjects among folk painters were Noah's ark and the story of the prodigal son.

Sketches, Doodles, and Odds and Ends

Folk artists have a passion for painting and drawing anything and everything. People, landscapes, and ships are not the only common subjects. Artists are naturally curious, and many try to draw nearly everything they see. Artists sketch and doodle all the time. In fact, most people at least occasionally doodle or sketch designs and pictures on notebook paper, scrap paper, and other items. While today's doodles may not yet be considered folk art, a doodle 200 years old is indeed folk art. Even sketches made in the classroom can be fascinating works of art.

This private art is often where fantasy worlds live, unrestrained by what "people will think." Unlike academic art that is meant to be shown in galleries and exhibitions, folk art is created mostly for private, not public, viewing. Doodles and sketches are the most primitive type of folk art, and are usually meant to be disposable.

Paint is not the only medium of choice for folk artists. Other materials include ink, pencils, markers, pastels, charcoals, chalk, crayons, or even a mixture of soot and saliva, which was used by James Castle (1900–1977). Canvas and artist's board are also not the only materials used to paint or draw on. Lined paper, scrap paper, newspaper, cardboard, metal, and wood have all been used in

The Peaceable Kingdom by Edward Hicks, 1849.

Activity
Reverse Painting on Glass

Originally imported from Asia into Europe, then from Europe into the United States, reverse painting on glass was very popular with folk artists during the 19th century. The technique involves painting with oils on the back of a piece of glass. The result is a delicate and shimmering work of art. Many of these works were set into wooden frames and placed above mirrors to make handsome wall hangings. Because the oils tend to separate from glass with time, most antique reverse-painted pictures are by now missing some paint.

In a normal painting, you can paint the entire sky blue first, then paint trees and other details over the sky. In a reverse painting, you cannot do that, because you will be looking at the painting from the other side, not the side you are painting on. In a reverse painting, you must paint the details first, and then add the background. You must also be careful not to overlap different colors.

Reverse-painted glass, early 19th century.

MATERIALS

Picture frame with glass

Oil paints of various colors

Paintbrush

Cotton swabs

Aluminum foil (optional)

Remove the glass from the frame. Decide what you want to paint; common folk art subjects included houses, landscapes, people, and flowers. Using the paintbrush, carefully paint the details of your subject. Any mistakes can be wiped away with a cotton swab. Now add the background color (black was common for portraits and still lifes, blue for the sky in landscapes). You can even silhouette some details in your painting by painting their outlines but leaving the detail unpainted. Let the paint dry. If you want to, you can cut a piece of aluminum foil the same size as the glass, and place it behind the entire glass before you frame it. This was often done in 19th-century reverse paintings to add extra sparkle.

How Old Is It?

View on the Hudson
by J. S. Jolly, late 19th century.

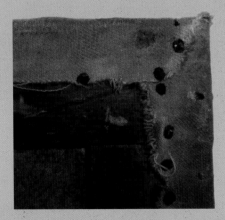

Detail of the stretched canvas of
View on the Hudson.

Early American folk paintings are only occasionally signed and dated. So how do the experts figure out how old these paintings are? They become art detectives and look for clues that will give them more information.

Antiques appraisers look for all types of clues, including a painting's subject matter, style, condition, and materials in determining a date and artist for the piece. Each factor alone may help to determine the age of a painting, but it is easier when all of the clues agree with each other. The styles of clothing and architecture and the types of vehicles depicted can all help date a painting.

This painting, signed "J. S. Jolly," was purchased for $26 from an antiques dealer. The painting is a landscape measuring about 13 inches high by 28 inches wide. Luckily, the subject matter is identified by the title, painted at the bottom right in black ink: *View on the Hudson*. To verify it, appraisers may check maps of the Hudson River in New York. They would see that there are numerous cliffs and mountains along the river's edge farther away from New York City. The painting also shows two sharp turns in the river.

Detailed maps of the Hudson River could be examined for any locations where there are at least two sharp curves in a row, and mountains right alongside them. There is a spot near West Point, New York, where the river looks similar to what is shown in the painting.

Style is difficult to evaluate because past styles can be copied at any time. Still, when combined with other factors, style can help. This painting is done in a primitive style that could be found during the 1800s. If a painting is signed, appraisers may try to find information about the artist in historical documents. This painter, J. S. Jolly, was researched in books and on the Internet, but nothing was found. New York state records could be checked, but just because the painting is of the Hudson does not mean that the painter lived there. Maybe he or she just visited there one summer weekend, or copied the scene from a print.

The condition of a painting often provides clues about its age. This painting's surface is covered with a coat of grime, and the paint is severely cracked. There is a tear in the canvas, on one of the trees along the riverbank where all the paint has flaked off. The back of the painting surface is stained (possibly from water damage) and the edges of the canvas are yellow and brown with age.

Even if the painting was stored in a damp attic, it would take 50 to 75 years to create conditions like these. Also, since it is pretty common to find American paintings from the 19th century on the market, an appraiser might guess that the painting is from the 19th century. The wood on this frame is old, and the age of the wood, canvas, and nails appears to be similar.

The materials used tell a lot about a painting's age as well. This canvas is hand stretched on a wooden frame. This is evident because the nails are spaced unevenly and are not in a straight row. The nail heads are not perfectly round, and because round wire nails were only introduced in the late 19th century, we know the frame is at least that old. Rust stains surround some of the nails. The handmade frame also indicates age.

Overall, these factors point to a date between 1860 and 1900. Painting became a more common pastime during the Victorian era of the late 19th century as people found time for hobbies, so it is likely that that is when the painting was made.

Activity
Make a Shadow Painting

There are plenty of other types of folk art in addition to what you will see in this book. Folk art is ever-changing because there are no rules. Even as you read these words, creative people around the country and the world are inventing new ways to make interesting artworks with their own talents and just a few simple raw materials. In this activity you can try your hand at shadow painting.

MATERIALS

Lawn chair

Small paintbrush

Black, brown, and deep green acrylic or poster paint

Large piece of cardboard or foamboard (at least 18 by 24 inches)

In either early morning or late afternoon on a sunny day, go outside and find a spot where there are trees, shrubs, or plants nearby. Look for the shadows being cast by these plants. Set up your lawn chair facing the sun and lean the cardboard up against the chair. Adjust the setup so that the shadow of at least a few leaves falls upon the board. Using the paintbrush, paint in the shadows of the leaves with the dark green paint, and the stems or branches with black or brown paint. When you are done, sign the painting at the bottom and write the date and time of day.

If you want to experiment with other shapes, find toys or oddly shaped objects in your house that might cast an interesting shadow.

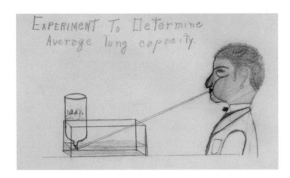

Experiment to Determine Average Lung Capacity by R. Patterson, 1924.

Friend Ella,
late 19th century.

folk art. The folk artist uses whatever he or she likes—there are no rules. Sometimes the artist is isolated and does not have access to art supply stores. The urge to create may come on suddenly, and the artist just grabs whatever is available.

Calligraphy

Calligraphy is a form of writing or drawing that produces beautiful, intricate, and artistic letters and drawings. Calligraphy originated with hand-written manuscripts that were slowly and carefully hand-lettered over a thousand years ago. Each style of lettering had its own name. These styles were the origins of the many different fonts, or typefaces, in use today. In those days there were no computers or even typewriters, so writing by hand was the only option. But until recently, relatively few people could read or write, and calligraphy was limited to a few experts.

Even in the 18th century and early 19th century, many Americans did not know how to write or read and did not attend school. Things changed rapidly by the mid-19th century, however, as the United States grew. A new importance was placed on schooling as villages grew into towns and cities. As the wilderness was tamed, schoolhouses flourished, and neat penmanship was one of the key points of education. Lettering was practiced not only by writing letters, but also by creating letters in needlework crafts such as embroidery.

Most people learned how to write using script (or cursive) lettering, but some wealthier people were able to continue their studies and learn an even fancier style of lettering. For example, an 1836 newspaper advertisement told of a man named Mr. A. L. Strong, who had been teaching penmanship for 12 years and who was now passing through Hartford, Connecticut, for a short while to offer calligraphy lessons to its citizens. The advertisement stated that "Mr. Strong, has just arrived, on his way to New-York, and begs leave to make a tender of his services, for a few weeks, to the Ladies and Gentlemen of this City . . . he confidently believes that for ease, rapidity, and elegance his penmanship is not surpassed" with a system that is "scientific and practical." A testimonial from the principal of the Greenfield High School for Young Ladies says that Mr. Strong's writing "quite surpasses anything I had ever seen or imagined."

A famous teacher named Platt R. Spencer (1800–1864) came up with his own system of writing that emphasized seven basic strokes of the pen and a 52-degree angle of writing as the keys to an elegant and flowing writing style. He published a book called *Theory of Spencerian Penmanship* as well as five workbooks. His Spencerian Pen Company sold the steel tips, or nibs, that were used to write with. Spencer has been called "the man who taught America to write" because his system became so wildly popular during the late 19th century. He explained that his intention was

> To present to the public a system,
> Plain to the eye, and gracefully combined,
> To train the muscle and inform the mind.

Handwriting exercise books were printed by the thousands, and avid students practiced and refined the art form of calligraphy. The idea, a common theme in folk art, was that a person did not have to be an artistic genius to produce delicate work. The secret was to stick to the principles outlined in the lessons. Every letter has its most basic elements. Calligraphy sought to add curves and swirls to those foundations, like fancy bows and ribbons on a present.

In 1888, the Zanerian College of Penmanship was founded in Ohio specifically to teach penmanship. Possible careers in drafting (drawing architectural or mechanical plans) or art were the goals of students who undertook this specialized training. Students practiced flourishes using a system similar to Spencer's. A common practice form was an elaborate, flowing version of a bird. The example shown on page 31 is most likely Zanerian and was done by C. E. D. Parker in 1898. Drawing a bird such as the one shown here helped students get a feel for their pens and practice the smooth curves that calligraphy letters required. The art of calligraphy also led to more elaborate decorative forms—drawings that depicted angels, birds, deer, and horses. These figures were drawn with flowing curves, and the outlines of the animals were filled in with hundreds of fine lines to create a unique type of drawing.

Calligraphy inspired a new surge in the popularity of drawing with pen and ink. Patience was required to make intricate art-

Activity

Draw a Spencerian Letter

The Spencerian system of writing produces smooth and graceful letters. To properly use the system, you have to master four different movements—finger movement, forearm movement, "combined" (finger and forearm) movement, and whole-arm movement. Try a few of the exercises shown here and see how you use muscles in different parts of your arm when you do them. Then you will be ready to try an actual example from Spencer's book on how to write a small "n."

MATERIALS

Lined paper

Pen or pencil

"Height one space [one line], width three spaces [three times the height of one line]. Begin on base line, and ascend with a left curve on connective slant, one space; turn short and descend with a straight line on main slant to base; then unite angularly and ascend with a left curve on connective slant, one space; again turn short and descend with a straight line on main slant to base; finally turn short and ascend with a right curve on connective slant, one space. Let the curves be equal, the turns equal, and the straight lines parallel."

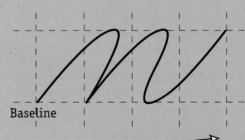

Baseline

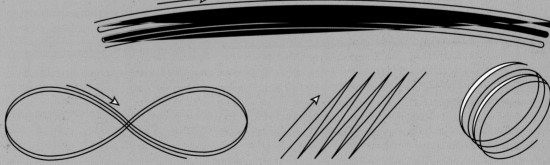

29

works where hundreds of flower petals had to be drawn, with no margin for error. The 19th-century ink drawing for Friend Ella shown on page 28 is a highly detailed work of art with an angel frolicking amid more than 30 flowers, vines and leaves, and a painstakingly drawn butterfly. The artist obviously used a very finely pointed pen to create the delicate line work.

Calligraphy is still used today for wedding invitations and other formal occasions, but the importance of carefully done, beautiful handwriting faded with the invention of the typewriter and the personal computer. Only a few people still practice the fine art of calligraphy on a regular basis.

Friendship and Autograph Albums

The last days of the school year bring a mixture of emotions for students—happiness that school is finally over, but sadness that they may not see many of their friends for a long time.

Drawings and inscriptions in autograph albums, yearbooks, and friendship albums are a way for kids and young adults to show their support and love for one another as they move forward in life. Often, these entries are humorous or profound poems or phrases that are meant to entertain or advise the owner of the album. Fancy calligraphy and colorful little pictures sometimes adorn these albums. The purple flowers and delicate bird shown on page 32 were both drawn in the autograph album of Cora L. Fiske, originally of

Pennsylvania, who attended Cazenovia Seminary in Cazenovia, New York.

These two short verses, written in 1881, also appear in the album. They give wishes that Cora should find a husband.

> Sailing down the river of life
> in your little canoe
> May you have a happy time
> Plenty of room for two.

> May you through life remain the same,
> Unchanged in all except your name
> Is the wish of your friend and classmate.

Others that appear in the album are slightly humorous:

> This remember when I am dead,
> Be sure you are right then go ahead.

And here's an entry by Cora herself:

> For fear that I should make you laugh,
> I'll only leave my autograph.

The reason for all the fancy script and ink flourishes is simple—most people want to make a good impression and be remembered kindly by their friends. These drawings were created with pride and made to be kept and treasured.

Fancy lettering or inked sketches can also be found in letters, journals, and diaries. During World War II, American soldiers sent millions of letters to their families and friends at home. These sometimes contained detailed drawings, especially for Christmas, birthdays, and other holidays.

Watercolor of a mansion, from a friendship album, mid-19th century.

Calligraphy Bird

The bird symbolized peace, love, and good luck and was therefore one of the most popular subjects for folk artists. Drawing its graceful curves was a nice way to practice calligraphy strokes. In this activity, you will practice the basic strokes and flourishes necessary to draw a calligraphy bird. The calligraphy pen nib (the tip) is specially shaped so that when you draw horizontally you will get a thick line, and when you draw vertically you will get a thin line. The transition from thick to thin is accomplished with a slight turn of the pen angle.

MATERIALS

15–20 sheets of white paper, 8½ by 11 inches
Few sheets of newspaper
Small bottle of India ink (1 ounce)
Calligraphy pen with 1/16-inch-wide nib

Find a place to work where you can lay down the newspaper. The spot you pick should be a hard, flat surface. After you have spread out the newspaper, lay two sheets of white paper on top of it. Use one sheet for scrap and the other for your drawing. Open the bottle of India ink and dip the tip of the calligraphy pen in for a second. When you remove the pen, the nib will be holding a small amount of ink. Draw a line on the scrap paper and see how writing with the pen feels. Those who use these pens know that the first line drawn after dipping the pen will be too inky, so a scrap piece of paper is used to get some of the excess ink out of the nib. When you feel like you have a nice, smooth line without too much or too little ink, try to draw flourish 1 on your good sheet of paper. If you mess it up, take another sheet and try again. Try flourishes 2 and 3. When you run out of ink, dip the pen again and draw a line on the scrap paper until the excess ink is gone.

Flourishes 4, 5, and 6 are also thick lines. Next comes flourish 7, the tail feathers. These are a series of smooth lines that curl downward. Flourish 8 is thin tail feather lines; hold your pen so that you write with the thin edge. Now try a few extra flourishes (pick from 9, 10, or 11). Finish the drawing by signing your name and dating it at the bottom.

Calligraphy bird by C. E. D. Parker, 1898.

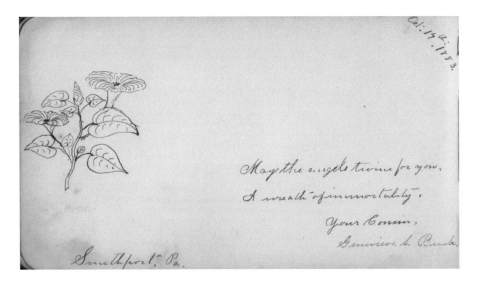

Vine with flowers in Cora Fiske's album
by Genevieve Bush, 1883.

Calligraphy bird in Cora Fiske's album
by A. L. Woods, 1884.

Tokens of Love

Both love and friendship inspired many works of folk art, but only love inspired both tears of happiness and sobs of desolation. Men and women through the centuries have been pouring their hearts out in the form of drawing and paintings, tokens of their love and affection. Some are simple drawings, while others are elaborately colored paintings. In the days before greeting cards, it was not so simple to find a preprinted card that expressed a person's exact feelings. While pretty store-bought paper valentines did exist, there was not a big selection of them, and they were expensive, so many sweethearts preferred to make their own love tokens.

In the mid-19th century, courtship was not as relaxed as it is today. Notes and letters might be exchanged for some time, with a limited number of dates that might consist of a few acceptable activities such as a stroll through the park or a night at the theater or opera. A man who courted a woman was expected to make some declaration of his intentions to her parents—was he planning to ask for her hand in marriage?

When a love relationship was ending, or was very intense, sentimental words of heartbreak or potential heartbreak might also be said through pictures and words. The valentine/farewell on page 34 shows a lovely young girl surrounded by flowers, and features the following lines:

Howard Finster

The Reverend Howard Finster was perhaps the best known living self-taught/outsider artist of the 1980s and 1990s. Born in Alabama, Finster was a Baptist preacher turned artist. Religion played a big role in his art, and many of his works feature images or words relating to the Bible. Since the 1960s, he worked at a place in Georgia he called Paradise Gardens, which he filled with his sculptures, paintings, and assorted junk.

As his fame spread, Paradise Gardens attracted many visitors. He charged admission, and visitors could browse, meet and talk to the artist, and purchase his works. During the 1980s, Howard Finster designed album covers for the rock groups R.E.M. and Talking Heads, which helped spread his fame around the country. Finster was always very prolific, rapidly churning out paintings. By the time he became sick and could no longer work in 2000, Finster had made more than 40,000 artworks, each one numbered sequentially.

But Howard Finster was not the only artist in the family. He encouraged his five children to paint. His daughter Beverly began doing sketches during the 1980s and was encouraged by her father, who loved her art and said she was the best artist in the family. Two of Finster's children and three of his grandchildren are also making art. In March 2000, Beverly decided she wanted to continue for her father by recreating some of his original designs. She spoke to him about it and he loved the idea. Because she always felt close to her father, it seemed natural. She continues to make Howard's designs in addition to making her own.

Beverly Finster says that as a child, she had no idea her father would become famous. "He never considered himself famous. He didn't want to be. He said that God should have all the fame, not people." Beverly Finster carries on the Finster torch and oversees her father's legacy. Besides that, she also sells her art and that of dozens of other folk artists. She is humble about her role, stating, "I'm just the gatekeeper."

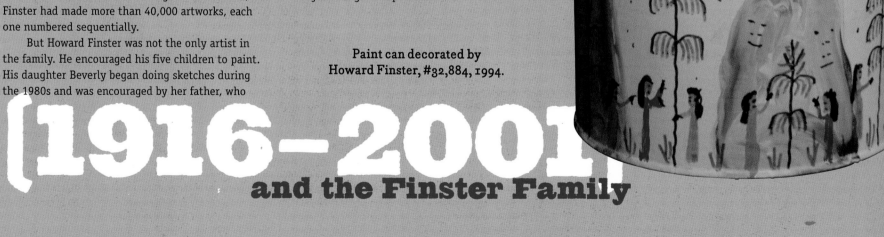

Paint can decorated by
Howard Finster, #32,884, 1994.

[1916–2001]
and the Finster Family

Pen-and-ink love token drawing with verse,
mid-19th century.

Some love the dark and raging sea
And some the citty's bustling hum
Resting their hopes on grand display;
And others a quiet mountain home
Had I but the pledge of thy constant heart
All else I would joyfully bid depart

Silhouettes

Costing a small fraction of the price of a painted portrait, having a silhouette made is an affordable way to get a likeness of oneself or a loved one. Silhouettes are not actually painted or drawn, but are cut out of paper. Named after the unpopular and penny-pinching 18th-century French minister of finance Etienne Silhouette, silhouettes were most common from the late 18th century to about the mid-19th century, before photography became popular, but they were still being cut well into the 20th century and even today.

In a way, the silhouette cutter's job is more difficult than the portrait painter's. They have to capture the essence of a person only by using his or her profile, without any technological help. Silhouettes are usually cut from thin black paper and pasted onto a lighter-color paper background for contrast. Hollow-cut silhouettes are cut from white paper and then placed over a black background.

Silhouettes cut by Beatrix Sherman. Left to right: Mr. S. G. Whitney, cut at the Panama-Pacific International Exposition, 1915; a young woman, date unknown; Reverend William Armhold, "87 years young," cut in May 1916.

Folk Art and Tradition

Academic painting is not the only art arena where tradition matters. There would be no folk art if traditions were not passed down from one generation to the next. And traditions cannot just be handed over without explanation. Children must learn about their culture's traditions through stories. Christmas, Thanksgiving, and Independence Day mean nothing unless a person knows what they stand for.

Because most people could not read until recently, the fables, stories, and poems of long ago were not written down, but were preserved through paintings and mosaics and through an oral tradition of one generation telling stories to the next. Eventually these stories were written down for posterity. Among the oldest written stories are the fables by the Greek writer Aesop, *The Odyssey* and *The Iliad* (which date back more than 2,000 years) by Homer, various stories from the Bible (also more than 2,000 years old), and the Mother Goose rhymes, some of which can be traced back at least 500 years. Other stories, such as those about George Washington and the founding of the United States, are more recent but are also extremely popular with folk artists.

Many works of folk art are based on these ancient stories, legends, or traditions. Some stories were taught in school; others were told at bedtime. Legends and true stories sometimes combine in the mind of a folk artist to create an original work of fantasy.

The most talented cutters took only a few minutes to create their works, and over a lifetime they created hundreds or even thousands of silhouette cuttings. One man claimed to have created 20,000 silhouettes in his career. There were no paints, canvases, palettes, easels, varnishes, or brushes to worry about, just paper and sharp scissors. There were no real "tricks," just an uncanny ability to use scissors to capture the essential features of a person's profile. Was the nose pointy? Was the brow protruding or receded? Was the chin jutting? What shape were the lips? How did the hair look?

The best-known silhouette cutter of the 20th century was Beatrix Sherman (1891–1975). She first began to cut silhouettes in 1915 at San Francisco's Panama-Pacific International Exposition. Sherman soon became famous for her precise and beautiful silhouettes. By 1918, she was cutting silhouettes of Hollywood stars and United States presidents. In 1922, she cut a silhouette of Arthur Conan Doyle, the creator of Sherlock Holmes, as he visited Atlantic City, New Jersey. She also silhouetted the aviator Amelia Earhart and the magician Harry Houdini. In 1939, she could be found cutting silhouettes at the New York World's Fair. Over the course of her career she silhouetted every president from Theodore Roosevelt to Lyndon Johnson. But Sherman was not just an artist to the stars. She cut portraits of countless average people of all ages just as willingly as she did of royalty and business tycoons. Sherman made two cuttings of each sitter, and she usually asked her subjects to autograph one for her to keep.

Memorial Pictures

During the early 19th century, women were expected to lead their families in mourning upon the death of a loved one. Girls who attended school were taught to read, write, sew, and paint memorial pictures. These paintings often showed people dressed in black and standing next to a tomb in a churchyard. Common death-related images that appeared in these paintings were the willow tree and the urn. The name of the person who was being mourned appeared on the tomb or elsewhere in the painting. One 1815 painting is dedicated to a woman who died in 1813, but the painting also has gravestones showing two children who died in 1793 and 1774.

Some of these pictures were embroidered rather than painted, and some were done in a combination of embroidery and painting. After the death of George Washington in 1799, memorial pictures for the beloved first president were common. Washington was so well liked that memorials were still being created decades after he died. By the mid-19th century, however, the memorial picture craze was over. Other mourning keepsakes, such as pieces of jewelry and keepsakes created with "plaited," or braided, locks of a loved one's hair, were created during the Victorian era of the mid- to late 19th century.

The Decorative Arts

The world is full of ordinary and practical objects. A folk artist takes these plain objects and makes them beautiful by decorating them with designs that celebrate in vivid colors and patterns and the many symbols, shapes, and natural wonders from around the world.

People have been using symbols and patterns in their drawings and designs for thousands of years. Both geometric designs, such as circles, squares, and triangles, and more abstract designs

were used all around the world in ancient times. These early designs were inspired by objects people observed in the natural world, such as the sun, the moon, the stars, and flowers.

The first forms of writing relied upon the use of symbols. For example, the ancient Mesopotamian cuneiform, meaning "wedge-shaped," and Egyptian hieroglyphics were both forms of writing that used pictures to symbolize animals, events, and other things. Ancient Egyptian art, found on the walls of tombs, contains colorful images of people and mythical creatures along with other pictographic symbols. In early Christian writings, the star symbolized birth, the infinity sign (a sideways "8") symbolized marriage, and the cross symbolized death. Each symbol was used for a reason. For example, the star might have been used to represent the star of Bethlehem that was said to have appeared when Jesus was born. The marriage symbol is two intertwined loops, symbolizing how bride's and groom's lives become intertwined when they marry.

Different cultures had different traditions of decorating. The decorative arts in colonial America, for example, relied heavily upon German, English, and other European decorative traditions.

Fraktur

For as long as there have been books, there have been colorful decorations that accompany their text. For over a thousand years and until the 15th

Illuminated manuscript, 1484.

century, books were hand-lettered by monks called scribes. The monks lived in monasteries and were committed to a life of prayer. They were usually more educated than the rest of the population, and they could read and write Latin and other languages. Naturally, neatness was crucial to their work of lettering. Each scribe had his own style, and even the same monk would not be able to duplicate his writing exactly the same way every time. Early manuscripts were truly unique works of art.

Some hand-lettered books were also illustrated with beautiful pictures and complicated designs of brightly colored inks. These books were called "illuminated manuscripts" because of their vibrant colors, including a yellow made with real gold, which practically jump off the page. The first letter or word on a page or in a chapter was often "rubricated," or outlined in red ink. In fancier manuscripts, these letters were drawn with fancy shapes and designs that represented life, death, love, and other elements of the human experience.

The most famous example of the beautiful art of illuminated manuscripts is *The Book of Kells*, an Irish masterpiece done in about the year 800. The book, currently on display in a museum in Dublin, Ireland, contains the four gospels of the Bible, each decorated with much colorful ornamentation. Religious and historical books were the most common category of illuminated manuscript.

The invention of the printing press in 1454 soon changed everything. For 50 years after that, colored inks were still used by hand to highlight

Fraktur in Franklin Township, Pennsylvania, family Bible by John Kruse, 1877–1884.

Detail of Gothic typeface, 1484.

Detail of Gothic typeface, 1484.

certain letters and make decorations on pages, but by the early 1500s, decorations and designs were inked into a "woodcut," a piece of wood carved with a design, or an "engraving," a piece of metal etched with a design, and printed using the printing press. The illuminated manuscript became obsolete.

Of course, the pictures were only a small part of books. Text filled most pages of the average book. Since only a small fraction of the population could read, let alone afford to purchase a book, during the Medieval and Renaissance years (500–1600), these books were only available to a select few people such as scholars and priests. While today's paperbacks are quite disposable, early books were not simply read and thrown away; they were treasures meant to be kept with pride. Early paper was also thicker and more durable than the paper used in today's books.

The style in which text was lettered differed by the place and time that the book was written. Many different styles, or typefaces, of lettering were in use between A.D. 1000 and 1600, including Caroline, Textura, Uncial, Rotunda, Gothic, Humanist, and Italic. A computer's word processing program may have some of these same fonts,

which have survived more than 500 years. One particular lettering style was favored by the Germans of the 16th century. Called "Fraktur," it was based on Gothic-style, sharply angled letters that gave the text a fractured or broken look, hence the name. This style of lettering was so popular that it was used in most German books until the end of World War II.

The form of folk art known as Fraktur is a direct descendant of both illuminated manuscripts and the Fraktur typeface favored by Germans. Though the handmade book was obsolete by the 16th and 17th centuries, hand lettering in Fraktur style, accompanied by colorful designs, was alive and well until the late 19th century. The Germans living near the Rhine River in an area known as the Palatine adorned works on paper and many everyday items with colorful drawings and designs featuring birds, tulips, and hearts. The Fraktur style of writing, along with these associated German designs, both became known simply as Fraktur.

By the early to mid-1700s, war, poverty, and hunger were causing thousands of Palatinites, as they were known, to emigrate to the colonies of America. Most of these early German settlers wound up in the colony of Pennsylvania. The German settlers were known as Pennsylvania Dutch. While they enjoyed their new lives in the land of opportunity, they held on to many of their old-world traditions.

Many religious groups fled Europe for Pennsylvania because of its religious freedom. One of these groups was the Schwenkfelders, a group founded by Caspar Schwenkfeld just after the

They Aren't Dutch

The Pennsylvania Dutch are sometimes confused with actual Dutch people from Holland. In fact, use of the word Dutch was a mistake, a misspelled English version of the German word *Deutsch*, which means German. The Pennsylvania Dutch have also been often confused with the Amish and Mennonites, small groups within the Pennsylvania Dutch population that have their own religious beliefs and cultural traditions, such as their plain manner of dress and their refusal to use modern technology.

Protestant Reformation began in the early 1500s. The Schwenkfelder style of Fraktur is perhaps the most loved among folk-art collectors.

First and foremost among the traditions of the Pennsylvania Dutch was the use of colorful designs and Fraktur in their decoration of certificates, documents, and items of furniture. A common theme, or motif, was the tulip, which symbolized faith. Here are some of the many ways in which Fraktur was used:

Student honors. School teachers sometimes used hand-drawn Fraktur certificates to reward the best-behaved and smartest students.

Birth, baptismal, and marriage certificates. These were some of the most common items on which Fraktur was used. The earliest Frakturs were all completely hand-drawn and painted. Local publishing companies caught on to the craze by the early 19th century and printed blank certificates to be hand-colored and filled in by their users or hired artists. Angels were commonly shown on these certificates. Though these certificates are known as fraktur, the names written on them were not always done in fraktur style, but sometimes in script.

Bookplates and bookmarks. By the 18th century, chances were good that an average family owned some books. Decorated bookplates and bookmarks were small but beautiful reminders of how treasured books were.

Records in the family Bible. These Bibles were sometimes hefty in size and weighed more than a couple of phone books. Fraktur was done in them by the people keeping the records or by a hired artist. In between the Old and New Testaments in these old Bibles were usually a few pages to record births, marriages, and deaths of the family that owned the Bible. The examples shown here are signed by an artist named John Kruse. There are flowery decorations and an angel's head drawn around some of the lettering. The marriage record and the first three birth records were done by Kruse, but it appears as though someone else did the bottom two records. The person drew in red ink and tried to copy Kruse's style, but did not possess quite as fine a talent. The designs shown here illustrate the original meaning of Fraktur—broken or angled lettering.

Fraktur flourished in Pennsylvania, Maryland, Ohio, and other eastern states until the end of the 19th century.

Painted Furniture

The essence of the decorative arts is taking an everyday object and transforming it into something beautiful. Fine examples exist of otherwise ordinary chairs and trunks that have been decorated with vivid Fraktur designs. These were sometimes given as wedding presents to German-American couples. Painted furniture was first covered in a single background color of paint, and then a design was applied with other colors. Painted furniture was a way to put a little color into the house in the days when not everyone could afford wallpaper or stenciling. It was also a way to hide the not-so-attractive appearance of cheaply made furniture and inexpensive wood. High-quality furniture was not painted.

The chair shown here is one of a set of four that were painted pale gray-blue first, then bright red, then black. After the black paint was applied, each chair was given a different leaf or flower design in green, red, and mustard colors. The three layers of paint prove that the chairs were not originally sold with the painted design, but were altered by their owner. More proof of amateur painting is a splash of paint that spilled onto the bottom of the cane seat during the decoration process. By the time this chair was painted, around 1900, painted furniture such as this could be found in many locations in America besides Pennsylvania.

Other methods of painting furniture include grain painting and special effects painting. The grain is the pattern of lines in a piece of wood. Grain painting involves the painting of brown, black, or red lines to make one type of wood look like another, more expensive type. Other tricks include painting knotholes on wood and using marbling or sponging effects to create a visual treat. One common recipient of this treatment was the useful 18th- and 19th-century piece of furniture called a chest over drawers. This item combined the easy access and large storage space of a chest with the convenience of drawers by making the top part of the piece a chest and the bottom part one or two drawers.

Paint-decorated chair, circa 1900.

Paint-decorated washstand, probably New York State, circa 1850s–60s.

Rewards of Merit

Free public school in the United States only became a reality in most places during the 19th century. Students who were well behaved or who performed their assignments well were likely to receive a small rectangular slip of paper known as a reward of merit. Though they were just small tokens, these rewards were supposed to encourage good behavior by giving students recognition and a pretty keepsake.

Rewards of merit were usually decorated with preprinted black-and-white engravings of flowers, children reading or playing, ships, birds, or other

Activity

Sponge-Paint a Stool

Many effects can be created using a few simple tricks. One of the easiest tricks is using a sponge to create a visually interesting marbled effect. This effect is found on painted furniture going back to colonial times. In this activity, you can experiment with sponge painting.

MATERIALS

Sheet of sandpaper

Small unfinished wooden stool, doll's chair, or other wooden item (available at crafts stores and unfinished furniture stores)

Acrylic paints of various colors

Paintbrush

Package of two or more kitchen sponges

Paper towels

Scrap wood or cardboard

Smooth any rough spots on the stool with the sandpaper. Pick a color to serve as your background, and paint the entire stool that color. Let it dry. Squeeze a swirl of another color paint onto a sponge. Now fold the sponge in half for a second, so that the paint is spread fairly evenly over the sponge's surface. Dab the sponge once onto a piece of paper towel to get the excess paint off. Now gently press the sponge onto a piece of scrap wood, then take it off. When you are satisfied with your pattern and color, start sponging the stool. If you want to, you can mix colors or apply one sponging over another for a different effect.

Reward of merit, circa 1870s.

designs. These designs were often hand-colored or painted before being given to the star pupils. Popular colors included vivid reds, greens, and yellows. The names of the student and teacher were neatly written by the teacher in ink on the lines provided. The example seen here is hand-colored, and it measures about 3½ by 2¼ inches. It is made out to young George Marshfelder from his teacher, Mary McMany. It likely dates back to the 1870s.

Sometimes rewards of merit were completely hand-painted stencils or decorative paintings. They contained more detailed descriptions of what the student had done to deserve the award. Amazingly, many of these fragile paper awards have survived through time and still exist today.

Teachers continued to give out rewards of merit for performance and attendance after the 19th century, but the hand-painting and coloring disappeared as classes became larger.

41

The Hex Sign

Nineteenth-century Pennsylvania Germans were very interested in decoration. Their love of colorful design extended beyond paper, pottery, and furniture. Sometime during the mid-1800s, the Pennsylvania Dutch began to paint circular symbols called hex signs onto their barns, sometimes as many as eight of them per building. There is disagreement about what these symbols mean. Some experts believe that they were meant to ward off witches and evil spirits, while others feel certain that they were made just for decoration. There are also those who think that the word *hex* comes directly from the German word *hexe*, meaning witch. Others think the Germans may have originally called these designs *sechs* in reference to the six-pointed stars that were featured in them, and that Americans misunderstood and thought they were saying *hex.*

We may never know the true origin of the name, but hex signs were probably made for a combination of both reasons—beauty and superstition. The symbols commonly found in hex signs, stars and rosettes, have been used by people for thousands of years and have religious significance. They are also supposed to bring good luck. The hex sign is sometimes thought of as being strictly an Amish custom, but in fact, the majority of hex signs on Pennsylvania buildings are located north of Amish country in Berks County.

The mid-20th century saw an explosion in the popularity of the Pennsylvania Dutch country as a tourist spot. Americans realized that the little section of Pennsylvania was special and interesting, and the hex sign became more widely known around the country. It has been used in advertisements for everything from egg noodles to pretzels. Local Pennsylvania artists began making hex signs on masonite board, making it possible for people to purchase and hang them on their own homes, barns, or garages. One of the pioneers of this process was an 11th-generation Pennsylvania German named Jacob Zook. He was the first to develop a silk-screen process to apply his designs to circular boards in a more efficient way than hand-painting each one. Silk-screened hex signs incorporated even more designs and often featured birds and hearts as well as rosettes and stars.

Pennsylvania Dutch hex sign,
mid- to late 20th century.

Hand-painted hex sign by R. Rossman,
early to mid-20th century.

Painting of a bird and flowers,
mid-20th century.

Activity

Make a Hex Sign

The lasting popularity of the hex sign must have something to do with its bright colors and pretty designs. Hex signs make one think pleasant thoughts of quiet farms, fading red barns, and wide green fields with grazing cows—a simpler way of life.

If you don't live near Pennsylvania or can't find a hex sign at a local garage sale, you can always make your own hex sign.

MATERIALS

Pencil

Compass

Square piece of very thin wood, foam board, thick cardboard, or poster board

Ruler

Green, blue, yellow, red, and black poster paints

You can make your own design, or you can try to duplicate the real hex sign shown here. To start, use the pencil and the compass to draw a large circle on the wood or board. Here are a couple of suggestions on how to proceed next:

Use the ruler to draw a diamond inside the circle. Using the compass, draw another circle inside the diamond. Now use the ruler to divide the inner circle into eight slices (like a pizza). In the very center of the circle, draw an eight-petaled flower.

Instead of a flower, you can use the ruler to draw a six-pointed star inside the circle. Draw a scallop-edged border around the outer circle.

Another idea is to use the compass to draw a smaller circle within the big circle. Decorate the smaller circle with a six-pointed star at the center and small hearts around the inner edge.

Now paint in the various portions of your design, being careful to stay within the pencil guidelines.

Watercolor of a bird and flowers, mid-19th century.

A commonly used bird is a fancy rendering of the *distelfink*, the thistle-seed-loving goldfinch, which is a symbol of good luck and happiness. Two *distelfinks* together imply happiness in marriage. The tradition of Zook's designs is still being carried on in the town of Paradise, Pennsylvania. Because of their mass production, the hex sign can now be found in all parts of the country.

Besides appearing in Fraktur and on hex signs, the tulip, heart, flower, and bird designs of the Pennsylvania Dutch have turned up on almost every type of object imaginable. As Americans began to appreciate their culture, Pennsylvania Germans have responded by producing many items to sell to the outside world. Pennsylvania Dutch country may be the biggest folk art production center in the country, and Americans love its art because of its vivid colors and joyful designs.

Stencil practice designs, circa 1947.

Stencils

Many of the everyday household items that we take for granted now were in short supply in centuries past. Furniture in the average house was limited, and paintings, carpets, and wallpaper were expensive. People longed for a way to liven up their drab homes without spending a fortune on decorating. Many people accomplished this with stencil painting. Some did stencil work themselves, and others hired professional stencil artists, who traveled from town to town.

A stencil is a design or pattern that has been cut out from a piece of thick paper. The stencil is held up against a wall, a piece of furniture, or some other item, and paint is dabbed in. When the stencil is removed, a perfect, colored shape is left behind.

The stencil artist understood how a little color in the right places could brighten a room. Hearts, roses, and stars could be painted in a variety of colors, including blue, red, yellow, and brown. The stencil artist took a look around the house and then quoted a price for different levels of work. Some people had borders painted, small patterns repeating along the tops of the walls all the way around the room. Others had entire walls stenciled with larger patterns.

Common 19th-century stencils included birds, flowers, pineapples, strawberry vines, leaves, hearts, and geometric shapes. Though much stenciling was done by anonymous artists, the work of Moses Eaton, Jr. (1796–1886) and other New England stencilers is still well known today. The discovery of Eaton's stencil box after his death helped researchers identify his work in different locations in Maine and New Hampshire. In addition to being a stencil artist, Eaton was also a farmer. The money made by stenciling alone may not have been enough to support a person.

It is not easy to find original 19th-century stencils that are still intact. Over the years, many old homes have been demolished, remodeled, or repainted several times. Unfortunately, it is impossible to repaint a wall without painting over the stencils. Some 200-year-old houses have 10 or more coats of paint or layers of wallpaper on the walls. Nineteenth-century president Franklin Pierce's boyhood home had stenciling, but very little of the art remains today because of fading and repainting.

Stencilers still practice this art form today. In many cases, they use patterns taken directly from two centuries ago. Though wallpaper is now cheaper than stenciling, the unique, colorful, folk-art look of stencils can do more for a room than any wallpaper.

In addition to walls, stenciling is also done on chests and other pieces of furniture. To stencil a piece of furniture, many steps are required. After a piece is sanded, the item is painted with a background color. Then the stencil pattern is painted. After the decorative part is completed, many coats of varnish are applied, with a light sanding done between coats to ensure a smooth surface. Once the last coat of varnish is completely dry, the piece is then hand-waxed and hand-buffed to a glossy finish.

Activity

Make a Stencil

The key to success for stencilers was the quality of their stencils. Having a nice selection of well-made stencils reassured potential customers that they could trust the stenciler and would be satisfied with the results. In this activity you will make your owns stencil and try it out.

MATERIALS

Pencil

Several sheets of 8½-by-11-inch white card stock (80 lb. or heavier)

Needle

Pair of nail (manicure) scissors

Pair of small, straight-bladed sewing scissors

Transparent tape

Stencil brush or stencil sponge

Craft paint (a few different colors)

Draw or trace a pattern for your stencil onto the paper. Remember that the more edges and curves the design has, the more difficult it will be to cut. Use the needle to poke a hole through your design as a starting point for cutting out the stencil. Use the nail scissors to cut curvy areas, and the sewing scissors to cut straighter lines. Carefully cut out the design, using tape to repair any small mistakes you might make. Try to cut a few different stencil designs.

Now you are ready to apply the stencil. Position the stencil over another piece of the paper and, using a stencil brush or stencil sponge, dab paint over the pattern. Carefully lift the pattern away, and let the stenciled paint dry.

Theorem Painting

During the 19th century, the middle class of modestly wealthy people expanded greatly. With the Industrial Revolution and the expanding world economy, cities and towns doubled and tripled in population. Families were now able to afford decorative objects for their homes, and they could afford to take up hobbies such as photography and painting.

Some women took art lessons and bought sets of watercolors or oil paints, palettes, canvases or artist boards, and brushes. Others decided to create art without taking lessons, and many of these people purchased precut stencils instead of making their own. Stencil painting on paper was fun, and it was certainly less risky than attempting to paint the walls of an entire living room with stencils.

"Theorem painting," or stenciling on paper, was very popular with 19th-century women because it allowed them to create unique and beautiful paintings without any artistic training. Carefully cut stencils were used to create sharp and crisp edges that would otherwise only be possible with great patience and a very fine paintbrush. Each stencil was not for a whole painting's design, but for a specific part of the painting. Every leaf, bud, flower, or fruit might have its own stencil. Theorem stencils became quite sophisticated, so that the paintings often looked very realistic. Each ring of petals of a flower could be stenciled separately to create shading and toning that made the flowers look more natural. Sometimes flowers were shown half-wilted or still budding.

Theorem paintings were done on white or light-colored velvet or on heavyweight paper. Most 19th-century theorems have not survived well, especially those done on paper, which tends to yellow and become brittle. Theorems were done by average people and were mostly unsigned, but they represent a highly evolved form of American folk art. Very fine examples of theorem paintings can be worth a great deal. As a trip to the crafts store will prove, stencil painting is still popular today, and the stencils are now laser-cut for even greater precision.

Stoneware

Clay has been dug out of the ground, molded into usable objects, and decorated for thousands of years all across the globe. Of all the types of clay pottery, the one that is best known as folk art in America is called "stoneware."

Fired in ovens at temperatures of more than 2,000°F for several days, stoneware is one of the most durable types of pottery in existence. For this reason, many pieces of stoneware from the 19th century still exist today, making it readily available for collectors of American antiques. In their autobiography, antiques dealers and television's *Antiques Roadshow* stars Leslie and Leigh Keno remember that some of the first antiques they collected as kids in upstate New York were stoneware jugs.

The process involved in creating stoneware made it difficult for individuals to manufacture it themselves. Potteries found it most efficient to make hundreds or thousands of pieces at a time. The body of each piece was made on a pottery wheel, and the handles were made separately and applied. After the molded clay had dried, it was placed into an oven at high temperatures with other pieces, and a large amount of table salt was thrown inside the oven. At the high temperatures, the salt vaporized and combined with the silica on the surface of the clay to create a glossy but pitted glaze (sodium silicate) that feels like a grapefruit skin. The vaporized salt did not thoroughly coat the insides of the pieces, so a special mixture of clay and water, called "slip," was made and applied to the interior. The most common type of slip in America used a special clay found near Albany, New York. It is known as Albany slip. This brown coating is found in almost all stoneware crocks from the 19th century.

What qualifies stoneware as folk art are the decorations that were applied to the pieces before they were fired. Three basic types of design were applied: stamped designs, which were impressed into the wet clay; patterns cut into the clay with a sharp instrument and filled in with glaze; and designs slip-glazed directly onto the clay.

People with little or no training were employed to "paint" designs onto the dried but not yet fired crocks. They were restricted in their choices of paint colors because of the high temperature of the firing process. A shade of blue made with the mineral cobalt and known as cobalt blue was able to withstand the high heat well, so it was most commonly used. Designs included flowers, birds, animals, patriotic themes, and abstract swirls.

The most popular type of stoneware vessel made was the crock, a large and heavy container

"Fred Bellen" stoneware with cobalt-blue design, made in Glens Falls, New York, mid-19th century.

that could hold several gallons of food or liquid for storage or pickling. Other vessels included jugs, small crocks called butter pots, and cake pots. Stoneware bottles were also made. These held drinks such as ginger beer, an early form of ginger ale.

Many American stoneware potteries were located in the Northeast, especially in New York, where the Hudson River and the Erie Canal made it easy to transport both raw materials and finished stoneware. Even though the pieces were often appreciated for their colorful decoration, stoneware was made to be functional. When other, less heavy types of food storage containers became common in the early 20th century, stoneware faded in popularity. The availability of prepackaged foods also helped end the stoneware era by reducing the need for storing bulk quantities of food items.

By the end of the 20th century, stoneware had become a popular collectible. Good pieces of decorated antique stoneware can easily fetch several hundred dollars in today's market. Many stoneware decorators were not only talented, but also very creative. Their elaborate designs are a true example of folk art, and pieces that feature them are worth several thousand dollars.

Other Pottery

Stoneware is just one of many types of pottery and ceramics that were common in the 19th century. Many other types existed, and each piece might have been specially shaped, or decorated with a paint, glaze, or slip that would qualify it as folk art.

Slip-glazed warming stone from the Horace Hooker house in Connecticut, circa 1820.

Redware. Made of red clay, which gives its distinctive color, redware is very fragile. Still, the abundance of red clay in many areas around the country made this a common type of pottery. The 19th-century warming stone shown on this page is one of a pair that was found sitting in the oven of an old 18th-century house in Connecticut. These unique pieces weigh five pounds each, are eight inches square, and are decorated with a red-and-yellow slip glaze in what looks like a tic-tac-toe pattern. Stones such as these could be used to keep food warm or even defrost cold feet.

Sgraffito. A type of redware commonly used to make plates, sgraffito pieces are covered by a pale yellowish slip. A design is then scratched into the slip, revealing the darker reddish color of the clay beneath. Authentic 19th-century sgraffito is difficult to find today.

Yellowware. A type of pottery made of yellowish clay found in New Jersey and Ohio. Yellowware was used to make mixing bowls and custard cups, among other items.

Ironstone. Made using a white, fairly durable clay, ironstone was used to make plates, bowls, and other tableware items.

Spongeware. Pottery that is designed with the help of a sponge. To make spongeware, paint (usually blue, green, or brown) is applied with a sponge to the surface of the item before it is fired.

Rockinghamware. Pottery, usually yellowware, that has a brownish dripped- or splattered-looking glaze.

Preserving Folk Art

How can people make sure their folk-art treasures will last a long time and not deteriorate? Here are some tips for preserving folk art:

- Keep art in a place that has low humidity. Humidity can cause mold to form on organic materials such as paper, baskets, and cotton or wool textiles. Moisture also causes iron, tin, and some other metals to rust.

- Keep the level of humidity constant. Changing levels of moisture in the air can cause wood and painted surfaces to crack and blister.

- Avoid high temperatures. High levels of heat, especially when combined with high humidity, can mean disaster. Bacteria and other harmful microorganisms can thrive under these conditions.

- Don't expose the art to direct sunlight. Paper can become yellowed and brittle, and textiles faded, when exposed to bright light. Colored plastics can also fade, as can almost any dyed or painted item.

- Use acid-free paper and storage materials to preserve art.

- Remove paper clips or staples from artwork. These can leave nasty rust stains behind on paper after only a few short months in storage.

- Don't add glue or tape to the artworks. Old photos or scrapbook items that have been glued into albums can become damaged. Tape does not last long and can do damage to art.

- Keep smoke, chemicals, deodorant sprays, cleaners, and grease away from art.

- Handle art with care. Sweat, grease, or dirt on fingers can damage papers.

- Have a trained professional repair damaged art.

48

Toleware

Before the days of plastic storage containers and metal filing cabinets, where did people store their documents? Iron containers were out of the question, because they rusted too easily. Rust stains can damage paper, so important documents such as deeds were stored in tin-plated document boxes. Traveling tin sellers went from town to town, hawking their wares, which included document boxes, trays, and coffeepots. Plain tin was not terribly interesting to look at, so decoration was welcomed. Painting on tin, or "tole painting," was very popular in the 19th century. Toleware was also known as "country tin," because it was more likely to be found in rural areas than in cities.

Tole (from the French word for sheet iron) painting is a cousin of both stenciling and Fraktur. Most painted tin was first lacquered in a black or brown paint made with asphalt and known as asphaltum. This process was called "japanning" because it was similar to a method used in Asia.

After the lacquer was applied, colorful leaf and flower designs were painted onto the surface using oil paints. The basic paint stroke of toleware is a leaf shaped like a fat comma. This stroke was usually used as a border, with flowers painted inside the border. As in stenciling and Fraktur, symmetry is important in tole painting. As with stenciling, few artists signed their works, so there are just a few well-known tole painters. One was Ann Butler, of New York.

Commemorative postage stamps featuring Pennsylvania toleware, issued in 1979.

Tole painting is done freehand, without the aid of stencils. Mistakes made using oils are not so easy to fix, and tin is not like paper that can be discarded after a mistake. Tole painters had to be very good at their craft, especially if they hoped to sell their wares.

Folk or Fake?

Many modern folk artists use primitive methods and materials to make "reproductions," pieces that look old but are really new. Many materials, such as painted wood, can be "distressed," or made to look old. There are several ways to accomplish this effect, including flaking or sanding existing paint off some spots. Chemicals can help weather metals to make them look old. Modern artists also use materials such as antique buckets or weathered wooden shingles in their art, which gives their work a more old-time feel.

In order to figure out whether a piece is really old or has just been made to look that way, appraisers look at the piece carefully. They make a checklist of each feature that makes the piece seem genuine, and each thing that makes them suspect it is a fake. The toleware sugar shaker shown here is an example of a suspicious piece. Though it looks old, something about it "didn't feel right" to the author. When asked, the proprietor of the antiques store where it was purchased said that she was not sure how old it was. Could it be about 100 years old? the proprietor was asked. "Yes, it could be 100 years old," she replied.

Clearly, the shaker itself is not new. The rust is so severe that the top is rusted to the body. Most of the time, modern folk artists want to make a reproduction that is at least functional. This sugar shaker can't be used at all. There is also heavy paint chipping and rust damage to the top, handle, and bottom rim of the shaker.

The design is not characteristic of the 1800s, however. Pennsylvania Dutch-style birds are not commonly found on 1800s painted tinware (flowers and fruit were the most common designs). A modern artist might tend to use designs that were never used in original pieces. In addition, the quality of the painted design on the body of the shaker is surprisingly good. Why is the top so rusty and chipped, while the rest of the piece is in much better shape?

An appraiser tried to read the signature on the bottom of the piece: "Peter O———[illegible]." This was definitely not an antique and practically worthless, she said. It was done in a "colonial revival" style that was common during the 1940s, and was made popular by an artist named Peter Hunt. Although this piece is not his, as the last name of the signature begins with an "O," a quick check of Peter Hunt on the Internet revealed that there was another artist, named Peter Ompir, who also worked in the same style. The mystery of "Peter O———" was solved.

Peter Ompir (1908–1979) was a folk artist who lived in New York and Massachusetts. He painted on anything he could get hold of, especially old worn pieces of tin and other antiques. He used a special finishing process to age the paint's appearance. He was not trying to trick people; his style was different from the original 19th-century toleware, and his work was signed by him and sold as new. Ompir's painted pieces were very popular. Though it likely dates from the 1950s and is not from the 1800s, the piece is not worthless. Because the shaker was painted by a respected folk artist, it still has value. Peter Ompir helped popularize painting on tin for everyday people around the country. Though they imitate aspects of an earlier style, his works are considered folk art and are collectible themselves.

Toleware sugar shaker
by Peter Ompir, mid-20th century.

Activity
Create a Paper Cutout

A beautiful form of 19th-century folk art involved delicate paper. Called scherenschnitte *(the German word for scissor cutting), this art was practiced in Pennsylvania. One type of art made by cutting paper was love tokens, which involved adding colorful Fraktur designs to the cutouts. In this activity, you will make your own paper cutout.*

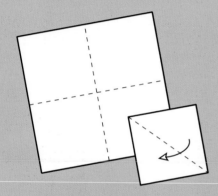

MATERIALS

- Square sheet of paper (at least 6 by 6 inches)
- Pair of small curved-edge scissors (manicure scissors)
- Pair of small straight-edged scissors
- Poster paints or markers (various colors)

Fold the sheet of paper in half, then in quarters. Next, fold it into eighths so that it forms a triangular shape. Use the curved scissors to cut a half-heart shape along the folded edge. Snip a few more curvy shapes, some going deep into the paper (an inch or two). Switch to the straight scissors and make triangular, square, and hexagonal cuts into the edge. When you are finished, open up the paper and you will see a beautiful design.

Paint a small red heart in the upper right corner of your *scherenschnitte*. While the paint is still wet, fold the paper in half, so that the outline of the heart comes off in the top left corner of the paper. Now you know exactly where to paint the heart in the upper left corner so it is symmetrical to the other one. Apply more paint to the first heart, fold the paper in half in the other direction, and repeat until you have painted hearts in all four corners. When the paint is completely dry, you can repeat this process with another design theme, such as a leaf, star, or flower. Your symmetrical *scherenschnitte* will look great when you are finished.

Feel free to experiment with the cutting. Try another one with more delicate cutting that curves and curls deeper into the center of the folded paper. Try still another one where you fold the paper into sixteenths instead of eighths. For even more dazzling results, try using gold or silver wrapping paper instead of plain paper.

Another common paper-cutting hobby was making paper dolls or animal cutouts and drawing or painting on them. Even though these "toys" were small and delicate, many have survived from the 19th century, tucked away in an envelope, diary, or scrapbook.

The Union Forever, paper cutout with watercolor, 1863.

Cut-paper horses with watercolor, mid-19th century

Fabric Sewn and Stitched

Since the frigid days of the Ice Age, textiles have played an important role in the story of human culture. Protective clothing is one of the most basic of human needs. The earliest clothes were simply animal skins that were thrown on like a wrap. With the beginnings of agriculture about 7,000 years ago, people discovered that certain animal fur (such as lamb's wool) and plant fibers (such as flax and cotton) could be woven into clothes. The first sewing needles, made of animal bone, also were invented

Cross-stitch sampler by Ruth Sellons, Long Island, New York, circa 1950.

ees use machines to make hundreds, even thousands of items every day. The finished clothes are then distributed to stores for people to purchase.

Today's methods are quite different from those used during the 18th century. Imported clothes were very expensive then. There were no machines to use to do the work; clothes had to be made completely by hand. Many people made all of their own clothes.

The first step was getting material. To do this, people grew cotton or flax plants, or raised sheep, from which they got wool. The cotton had to be picked, and the fibers were separated from the unusable parts. Sheep were sheared when their coats were thick, and the wool was gathered and brushed out.

Next, the cotton or wool fibers were spun together tightly into yarn on a wooden contraption called a spinning wheel. Spinning wheels used to be a common item in most households. The yarn made from the spinning wheel was then colored with dyes made from berries and other natural sources. After dyeing, the yarn was finally ready to be used to create fabrics and clothing.

Weaving

Weaving is the most ancient method of creating fabric. It is done on a "loom," a contraption that holds and stretchs the material being woven. Looms range in size from small laptop ones to

around this time. As people settled into agricultural villages and towns, textile making really blossomed, and included clothes, blankets, rugs, and sacks for carrying things.

From Plant to Blanket

How are clothes made? Today, most clothes are made in large factories, where dozens of employ-

large looms that take up most of a room. To weave a piece of cloth, strands of yarn are run in straight lines from the far end of the loom to the near end. These up and down strands are known as the "warp" of the fabric. Other strands of yarn are then woven over and under each of the warp strands, back and forth until an entire piece of cloth is created. These strands are called the "weft" of the fabric. This simple crisscrossing of hundreds or thousands of strands of yarn is what gives fabric its strength and helps woven items last a long time.

Patterns are woven into the fabric by changing the color of the yarn. During medieval times, weaving was used to create tapestries. These were large pieces of fabric that had designs of people and sometimes even epic stories woven into them.

Weaving was often done by men as a profession. For hundreds of years, each town in Europe had its own weaver. In Germany the village weaver was known as a *weber*. The Latin word for weaver is *textor*, which also means to build or compose. The English words text and textile are derived from the Latin word for weave.

Native American basket, probably New England, circa 1920s

Basket Weaving

Fabric is not the only thing that is woven from plant fibers. Since ancient times, certain plant leaves and stems have been dried and split into thin strips, then woven into baskets. These baskets have been used to carry food and personal items, as well as to decorate. Natural dyes can be used to create brightly colored patterns and designs.

There are a few basic basket types, including coiled and plaited. Coiled baskets are made by "sewing" small loops around the horizontal frame of the basket. Plaited baskets are made by weaving thin, flexible pieces of fiber together. Wicker baskets are plaited baskets that are made by weaving thick, stiff pieces of fiber together.

Basket making in America is a tradition with a long heritage. While the Shakers are known for their fine baskets of the 19th and 20th centuries, Native American cultures have been making baskets for thousands of years. Many of these beautiful creations have been preserved by the Smithsonian Institution. Today, Native basket makers are still active across the nation. Much of this artwork is made to sell to tourists to help bring money into their communities.

Knitting and Crocheting

Knitting and crocheting are two old methods of hand-creating sturdy and warm clothes and fabrics from yarn. Crocheting uses a single needle with a hook on the tip. The hook is used to catch and hold a loop of yarn while the needle goes through a second loop, and then is pulled through, leaving the second loop under the hook. Knitting uses two pointed needles from which the piece being made is strung. As with crocheting, the yarn goes around the needle and then is worked into the piece. Unlike weaving, knitting and crocheting were usually done by women. These skills were passed down from mother to daughter for generations. Practice was gained from the making of clothes, especially blan-

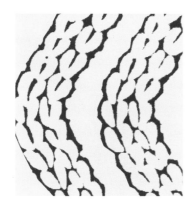

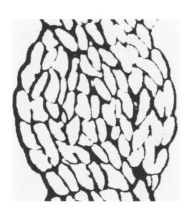

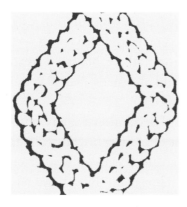

Three Aran sweater patterns: double zigzag, cable, and diamond.

kets, sweaters, scarves, gloves, and hats. Sometimes store-bought patterns were used, and other times people created their own designs. The popularity of knitting and crocheting fell after the mid-20th century, as more women entered the work force. Few had the spare time to make clothing by hand.

Sometimes in textile making, the stitch itself is a type of folk art. In the Aran Irish tradition, the fishermen of the 19th century wore heavy oiled woolen sweaters to keep them warm and dry against the cold, moist air of the rocky Aran Islands located off the western coast of Ireland. They knit into their sweaters a variety of stitches, each of which had a different meaning. The diamond stitch signified fame and fortune; the cable stitch meant safety and good luck when fishing; the double zigzag or ladder stitch signified the ups and downs of marriage; the honeycomb stitch signified hard work leading to success; the tree of life stitch meant family unity; and the double moss stitch symbolized good health. Each man wore a unique combination of patterns chosen by his wife. The story goes that if a fisherman died at sea, the pattern of his sweater was sometimes all a wife had to identify his body.

Folk Costumes

Some of the most obvious folk traditions of people throughout history involved their costumes. Each ethnic group had certain clothing styles and colors that were favored over all others. The fabric thickness, amount of skin coverage, and colors were sometimes determined by the climate of the area where the people lived; pale colors were favored by

Late 19th-century costumes from Dalmatia, an area bordering the Adriatic Sea.

people in hot regions, and more fabric and darker colors were used by people in colder regions. These costumes were complex, and they consisted of many items of clothing, often including stockings, shirts, pants, suspenders, skirts, vests, scarves, robes, belts, hats, and shoes. The costumes were often colorful, and many featured embroidered designs.

As time passed and more people moved into cities, only those left in the countryside really kept up the tradition of wearing decorative folk costumes. Folk costumes are still worn on special occasions in many places today, but the events are designed as much to draw tourists as to maintain folk traditions. The use of folk costumes contin-

55

ued to decline as millions of immigrants came from overseas to America. Though some people held on to their costume traditions for years after their arrival, as their children tried to become part of the American culture, many dropped the customs and traditional dress of their native countries so they would not stand out so much.

Lace

Lace can be made in a few different ways. One common method involves the use of a very fine-hooked crochet needle and very thin cotton yarn. Strands of yarn (usually white, but sometimes other pale colors) are interconnected in a delicate weave to make tablecloths, doilies, or edging for a piece of clothing. Lace making was more common before World War II, when women were more likely to be at home and have the time for such crafts. Patterns for lace were helpful, but they were not necessary for the skilled lace maker.

Much lace making did not require any special equipment, but some patterns required the use of a special wheel to create medallions, which were stitched together with thread. The wheel was the "form" around which the yarn was wound to make the round lace segments. Lace making was a way to capture dreams of "Old World" charm and distinction in America. Shown here is a one such pattern, called Octerette.

Detail of lace tablecloth, Octerette pattern by M. Leyden, circa 1940.

Needlepoint eagle by Eleanor Sullivan, 1980.

Embroidery and Needlepoint

For thousands of years, people have decorated their handmade fabrics with colorful designs. Throughout recent history, decorative needlework has been done on clothing, household textiles such as tablecloths and placemats, and other items such as handkerchiefs.

One type of decoration, called embroidery, involves the use of an often brightly colored thread called floss to create designs on a separately made piece of cloth. Though this folk art was taught to young girls all around the world, there are some towns that have become known for their distinctive embroidery. On page 5 in chapter 1 is a photo-

Butterfly hooked rug, wool on burlap, circa 1880.

to create a picture. The cross-stitch picture of an eagle seen here features "counted cross-stitch," meaning that the maker had to refer to a chart and determine the placement and number of stitches of each color of floss. Other kinds of cross-stitch include stamped cross-stitch, in which the pattern is stamped on the canvas fabric. Samplers are often done using a cross-stitch method.

Hooked Rugs

Wall-to-wall carpeting is very common today, but until recently it was unheard of. It was only the invention of synthetic fibers such as polyester and nylon that made it possible to carpet an entire home at an affordable price. Before then, most homes had bare wood floors, which got rather cold during the winter. Only the wealthier families could afford luxurious imported rugs and carpets, which were handmade in Europe and Asia. Early Americans were quite inventive, however, and they came up with a unique way to make their own rugs at a low cost.

Hooked rugs were made using a burlap foundation, the base onto which the rug fabric is woven. Narrow strips of colored fabric are pulled through the holes in the burlap with a wood-handled metal hook to create fabric loops that are very close together. This creates a dense pile, or surface.

Patterns for hooked rugs were available to purchase. These were usually simple geometric designs, such as circles, squares, or triangles, or floral or pictorial designs. Some rugs were made without a pattern. These original designs were

graph of a tablecloth from the town of Kalocsa, Hungary. Considered a national treasure, Kalocsa embroidery features very distinctive patterns and designs found nowhere else in the world. No two Kalocsa patterns are exactly the same in color or design, and exact symmetry is never found in this embroidery work. The joyful floral patterns seen in European embroidery were imported to America and used to decorate many items, including painted furniture and toleware, in addition to embroidered objects.

Needlepoint is embroidery that is done on canvas, usually to make embroidered pictures that can be framed. Cross-stitch is another type of embroidery. It uses stitches in the shape of an "x"

Samplers

In addition to learning to read and write, 19th-century schoolgirls were expected to learn to sew. Before the days of the electric sewing machine and inexpensive store-bought clothes, women needed to know how to use a needle and thread. Making samplers was a perfect way for schoolgirls to study the alphabet, numbers, and literature while practicing different sewing stitches and techniques. The pieces are called samplers because they include samples of different lettering styles, colors, pictures, and stitches. These girls had no idea they were making works of art, but each sampler had its own unique creative twists and charm that still have appeal today.

Using silk or cotton thread, a design was sewn in various colors onto a piece of linen. These designs usually included the letters of the alphabet in lower and upper case, sometimes in several styles. Most samplers also featured the numbers from zero to nine, and they sometimes included a favorite proverb or biblical or literary quote. These quotes sometimes took up the entire sampler, leaving no room for the alphabet or numbers. Many samplers are signed and dated. Sometimes they include the ages of the girls who made them, or the name of the place where they were made.

The example shown on this page was done by a girl named Maria Galvez. Young Maria was of Spanish descent, and she may have lived in San Felipe, California, or perhaps in Mexico or Spain. She dated her work September 1892. Hers is an example of the "Berlin work" of the late 19th cen-

often more complicated and less symmetrical than the pattern designs. The butterfly hooked rug, shown on this page, is an example of an original design. Notice that the antennae, wings, and eyes are different in shape and size on the left side than on the right side. As with most good folk art, these original designs possessed an invitingly warm and primitive look.

Farm animal feed sacks, made of burlap, provided an easily obtainable source for the base of a hooked rug. Old scraps of fabric that might otherwise be thrown away were perfect to use for the pile. Because of the odds and ends used for these rug materials, the finished products are not perfect in shape and have a scrappy look to them. A good hooked rug will seem primitive and charming, while at the same time sophisticated and meaningful, just like a folk painting.

Sampler sewn to a wooden backing, 1820.

a crown, a ladder, a bottle, an axe, a compass, a heart, a top, a harp, a wine glass, and a feather.

The second sampler shown is unsigned, but is dated 1820. Its charm is in its primitive appearance. Though it is faded and deteriorated with age, you can still see the work that was put into it. You can also see a few mistakes—proof that the girls sewing samplers were, of course, human, and were still learning to sew. The edges of the fabric were stitched to a very thin piece of wood long ago, maybe by proud parents for display purposes, or to help preserve the piece.

Made mainly by girls aged 8 to 13, samplers were most commonly found in England and in parts of the eastern United States. Teachers played a role in helping guide students in their stitchery. Common 19th-century images included birds, people, flowers, dogs, deer, urns, trees, and stately homes. Some samplers have little or no decoration, just several different types of stitches. These are called "stitch samplers." Victorian-era girls also made bookmark samplers, and they occasionally used punched paper (a sturdy paper with tiny holes punched throughout) instead of cloth on which to sew.

Other types of samplers include:

Buttonhole. These were made so that girls could practice the art of making buttonholes; remember that homemade clothes required buttons, and poorly made holes would rip with use. Practicing a thread-lined buttonhole helped girls to make more durable clothes.

Home Sweet Home. Some samplers have a home blessing or simply the words "Home Sweet Home" sewn on them.

tury, which featured bright new wool yarn colors not found in older silk thread samplers. The bright pink, orange, and yellow, along with the interesting subject matter, are not typical of the earlier samplers. Some of the unusual items found in this sampler are a parrot, a dog, butterflies, a shovel,

Activity

Make a Cross-Stitch Sampler

The importance of knowing how to sew has decreased because people rarely make or mend their own clothes anymore, but sewing can be a fun way to create your own folk art. Cross-stitch is great practice for sewing because it allows you to do the same small, efficient stitch over and over. In this activity, you will make a simple cross-stitch sampler.

MATERIALS

Markers in various colors

1 piece of blank needlepoint fabric (9 by 12 inches or smaller), purchased at a craft store

Pair of straight-edged scissors

Needlepoint yarn, in colors to match those of the markers

Large-eyed needlepoint needle

Using different-colored markers, draw the letters A, B, and C in a row, and the numbers 1, 2, and 3 in a row below the letters, on the needlepoint fabric. Draw a star to the right of the letters, and another to the left of the numbers. Leave at least a one-inch margin around the edges. Using one color of yarn at a time, cut a length of yarn, thread the needle, and sew over each letter and number as follows: Bring the needle up through the first hole in the color you are working on; push the needle down through the hole diagonally down to the left of it; then up through the hole one space over to the right, and down again through the hole diagonally above and to the left. When you have finished sewing one letter, tie a knot in the yarn from behind. Thread the needle with the next color of yarn. If you are doing a straight horizontal or vertical line, you can stitch all of the stitches in one direction first, then come back the other direction and stitch all of the opposite stitches (instead of doing each "x" separately). When you have finished with the numbers, letters, and stars, sew a border around the edge of your sampler, and sew your initials in one corner.

The Mennonites

Founded in Switzerland by Menno Simons during the 16th century, the Mennonites were an offshoot of the Anabaptist religion. As the movement spread across Europe, the Mennonites were persecuted. They welcomed the chance to migrate to America when William Penn proclaimed the territory of Pennsylvania as a place of religious freedom, and the first American Mennonite community was founded in Germantown, Pennsylvania, in 1683. The Mennonites are also known as the "plain" people.

They believe in adult baptism, and in a return to more traditional ways. They do not believe in modern technology, and they use only horse-drawn wagons and buggies to travel.

The Amish broke away from the Mennonites in 1693 and though the two groups share beliefs, they have different customs.

The Mennonites have survived well into the 21st century. A trip into Lancaster County, Pennsylvania, and a few other locations (Ohio for example) will reveal that their culture stil thrives.

This primitive-style painting, made using ink, watercolor, and paint on paper, gathers many of the characteristics of Pennsylvania Dutch country into one place, including a covered bridge, a barn with hex signs, farm animals, old colonial homes, and horse and buggies.

The "plain people" are known for their fine quilts of the late 1800s. Popular designs included a diamond inside a square, as well as fruit, flowers, baskets, and Joseph's Coat, a colorful design with bars that represent the different colors of the multicolored coat of the Old Testament Joseph. Although their beliefs call for "plain" living, quilting was one activity in which they allowed their creativity to emerge.

Untitled by E. Kimmel, mid-20th century.

and the Amish

Holiday. Christmas greetings and designs, such as candy canes, wreaths, and trees, can be found on some samplers, mostly mid-19th century or later.

The value of an antique sampler depends on its age, condition, and the level of detail in the piece. Aging has caused the linen of many of these old pieces to yellow. Areas of loss (patches where the fabric has deteriorated or is missing) to the linen are common in old samplers, as is evident on the 1820 sampler shown. Collectors and scholars prize American samplers that were done before 1800 and made by girls living in New England, because they tell us about colonial life.

Quilts

Today's garbage cans are filled with scraps of our lives—used and discarded bits and pieces of everything imaginable. If a pair of jeans have a rip, or a T-shirt has a hole, into the garbage it goes in a split second. Dresses, pants, and shirts are cheaper now than they have ever been. Factories and cheap labor have made clothes affordable, and disposable, for everyone; it is easy enough to buy a new T-shirt for a couple of dollars. But until the Great Depression ended in the early 1940s, this kind of behavior would have been unheard of except among the wealthiest of families.

In days past, if something ripped, it would be mended. If it ripped again, it would be mended again. Finally, when it was not wearable anymore, it might be cut into small pieces for use in a quilt or

Album quilt, eastern United States, 1840.

From simply being a way to recycle scraps of fabric, the quilt evolved into an art form. Quilting was done mainly by girls and women. Through the 19th century, women were not allowed very many ways to express themselves or their creativity, so quilt making was a welcomed opportunity to do so. Experimentation with colors and shapes led to an infinite variety of designs, and it is almost impossible to find two handmade quilts that are exactly alike. Many quilts use geometric shapes, such as diamonds, triangles, and squares, to create patterns. These patterns have very colorful names, such as "log cabin" (a series of squares within squares made up of "logs," or individual strips of fabric), "tumbling blocks" (three-dimensional cubes), "blazing star," "drunkard's path," which looks a little like a maze, "courthouse steps," "postage stamp" (small squares), "honeycomb" (hexagonal pieces of fabric), "crossroads" and "Irish chain" (crisscross patterns), "mariner's compass," "goose in the pond," "maple leaf," "basket," "lone star," and "spools." Many of these are difficult patterns that require an experienced quilter. Each tiny strip of fabric in these types of quilts must be cut and sewn precisely, or the pattern will be lopsided. Dozens of different fabrics are used to create a good quilt.

In the 19th century, books of quilt patterns were published so women could have a guideline to follow for the design, but fabric selection was always up to the quilt maker. Many women added their own unique twists to a quilt. For example, one 1880 quilt features pictures of soon-to-be President James Garfield and his vice president, Chester

a hooked rug. Recycling fabric was common, and a good seamstress knew how to make scraps into something beautiful and useful. These days, fabric for making a quilt is often purchased new, and there are thousands of different fabrics to choose from. During the 19th century, a quilt maker had only a handful of salvaged remnants. Still, a quilt was easier and cheaper to make than a blanket, which required yarn.

Activity

Sew an Album Quilt Square

The album quilt is fascinating because it involves many different people working together to make it. Each person provides a square for the quilt. Album quilts were often presented to a friend or relative who was moving far away, as a reminder of the friends and family left behind. A common theme is usually present throughout an album quilt, as in the example shown on page 62. When all of the squares have been made, they are stitched together to make the quilt. In this activity you will make an album quilt square.

MATERIALS

Sheet of tracing paper

Magazines or books with pictures

Pencil

Pair of straight-edged scissors or fabric shears

Fabric swatches (any type) or old clothes that can be cut up

Needle

Thread

Two 6-by-6-inch squares of solid-color fabric

5½-by-5½-inch piece of white felt

Think of a theme for your quilt square. Examples include: animals, the sea, food, and letters of the alphabet. Once you have picked your theme, pick the subject of your square (for a theme of animals, you might choose a horse, for example). Now you are ready to create your design.

Lay the tracing paper over a picture from a magazine or book, and trace it with the pencil. Next, cut the tracing out. You now have a pattern. Lay the pattern over a fabric swatch and cut out the same shape in fabric.

Using the needle and thread, sew the shape you have cut out to one of the pieces of solid-colored fabric. You can also cut out letters, numbers, or anything else you might want to add to the album quilt square. If you have trouble sewing the shape on, you can use fabric glue and glue it down instead.

Lay down the other piece of solid-colored fabric. Place the piece of felt on top of it, and place the piece of fabric (that has the design sewn onto it) on top of that. The felt will serve as the batting, or stuffing, for your quilt square. Now sew the bottom and the top pieces of fabric together at the edges so that the felt is inside.

Ask your family, friends, or classmates to make their own squares. You can lay all the squares next to each other and see what your album quilt would look like.

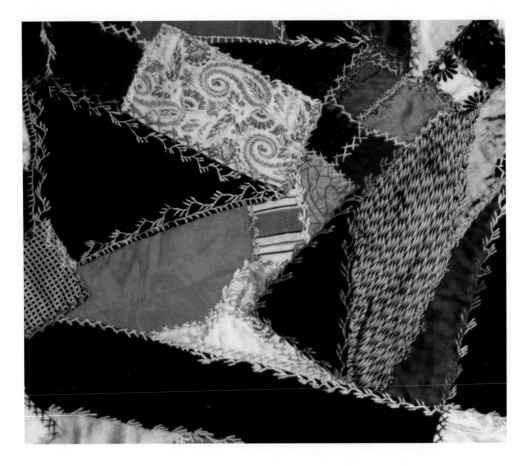

For a patchwork quilt, the pieces of fabric are sewn to each other with larger and more elaborate stitches, and then stitched to a foundation piece of fabric. There are dozens of patchwork stitches, including the "feather" and the "herringbone." A patchwork quilt is often like a puzzle, since the pieces sometimes have to be fit together to form a block, or square, of fabric, that can be joined to other blocks. The small crazy quilt shown on this page is made of only one block.

The original purpose of making a quilt was not to use up old scraps of fabric; it was to make a warm piece of bedding. A quilt is usually filled with "batting," or stuffing between the foundation fabric on the bottom and the quilt's designed top, to make it extra cozy on a drafty winter's night. The three layers provided extra insulation against the cold, compared to a blanket, which has only one layer.

The different layers of fabric in a quilt cannot simply be sewn together around the edges, though. If that were done, the three layers would bunch up and the quilt would be slowly destroyed with each use and washing. The layers must be quilted, or stitched together, in order for the quilt to hold up over time. Until the introduction of the sewing machine, this was done by hand. Stitches ranged from a very simple diamond pattern to fancy designs that enhanced the appearance of the quilt. Some communities held "quilting bees," during which one or more quilts were assembled and finished jointly by a group of women quilters.

There are many different types of quilts, including

Arthur. Another, made between 1885 and 1890, was dedicated to President Grover Cleveland's presidential campaign and inauguration.

Large quilts can cover an entire bed, while smaller ones, called coverlets, serve as bed or lap blankets. Quilts are usually made using one of two methods: appliqué or patchwork. Appliqué involves taking a background fabric and, using tiny, almost invisible stitches, neatly sewing small pieces of colored fabric onto it to create a pattern.

Activity

Design a Quilt

Quilting was one of the most popular leisure activities in America during the 18th and 19th centuries. The art of quilting was passed down from generation to generation. The wide variety of patterns and fabrics available allowed the quilt makers a lot of creativity. The actual process of making a quilt is long and difficult, and it often involves many hours of work to sew the pieces of fabric and batting to a large piece of fabric. Some quilts took many weeks or months to complete. In this activity, you will get to enjoy designing a miniature version of a quilt without having to spend too much time doing it.

MATERIALS

Pencil

Ruler

Piece of 8½- by 11-inch cardboard

Pair of straight-edged scissors or fabric shears

Fabric swatches or old clothes that can be cut up

Glue suitable for use on fabrics

8½- by 11-inch picture frame (optional)

Using the pencil and ruler, divide the cardboard into four equal parts. Use the ruler to draw the same design in each section. (See the sample pattern shown here.)

Cut the fabric swatches into small pieces that exactly match the size and shape of the pattern shapes you drew. Using the glue sparingly, paste the fabric onto the designs drawn on the cardboard.

When you are finished, you can frame your art and display it on your desk or a wall.

Wholecloth quilt. This is made with just a couple of pieces of fabric, and the main design might be the quilting stitches that hold the layers together.

Album, Friendship, or Presentation quilt. This type of quilt has blocks made (and often signed) by different women, and then each block is sewn to the body of the quilt, and the finished product is presented as a gift.

Mosaic quilt. This type of quilt is made from hundreds of small pieces of fabric, and it features geometric patterns that might have a dizzying effect on the eyes when viewed from afar.

Medallion quilt. This type of quilt has a large picture or design in its center.

Sampler quilt. This type has a different subject in each block. For example, a leaf, a bird, a geometric pattern, and a cross may appear in separate blocked sections of the quilt.

Crazy quilt. Imagine taking a whole bunch of differently shaped and colored fabrics and sewing them together into a wild abstract quilt. Crazy quilts are the most colorful and creative type of quilt, and they were very popular during Victorian times of the late 19th century. The rich colors and expensive fabrics of these quilts were a perfect match for the tastes of the times. Besides that, they were interesting to look at

and fun to make. In the patchwork crazy quilt shown on page 64, the maker has used purple, green, blue, black, brown, and burgundy velvet along with brown, green, blue, pink, and yellow silk or satin to create a rich-looking treat for the eye. She used large and fancy stitches of many bright colors of embroidery floss to hold the different pieces of fabric together, sewed them to a foundation, and applied a green velvet border. At one corner of the quilt she has sewn what looks like a sun and five red rays of sunlight. This actually represents a Japanese fan—Asian themes were popular during the late Victorian era.

Good quilts were durable, made to last a long time. That is why so many fine examples of old quilts still exist today. But quilting's popularity did not die out during the 20th century. In fact, the love of quilting in America is stronger today than ever before. Today's quilt makers have 200 years of patterns to pick through, as well as their own imaginations, to come up with what will eventually become tomorrow's treasured antique folk-art quilts. The latest craze involves creating gigantic quilts in honor of a worthy cause, such as remembering victims of AIDS or domestic violence.

Rag Dolls

If she was lucky, a 19th-century girl might get a very special present from a wealthy relative one year for Christmas. She might receive a finely made imported doll with pretty clothes and a "bisque," or porcelain, head. Though this new doll would receive a place of honor on her bed, the doll she would actually

Rag doll, late 19th century.

play with on a daily basis would still be the one that her big sister or mother had made for her out of scraps of fabric and yarn.

The rag doll, or cloth doll, has been around for hundreds of years. These dolls were easy to make. The body was made from pieces of simple cotton knit fabric (the kind a T-shirt is made from), and scraps of fabric were used for the stuffing. Yarn was used to make features on the face and hair for the doll. Additional bits and pieces of fabric were used to make dresses, hats, shoes, and other accessories for it. Details were not often found on rag dolls. The material made it difficult to portray fingers, toes, and ears. Nonetheless, these dolls have a certain personality to them.

Rag dolls became famous when a writer named Johnny Gruelle found an old rag doll in his mother's attic and thought it would make a good idea for a story. In 1918, *Raggedy Ann Stories* was published, telling of the adventures of the famous red-headed rag doll. Many more books about Raggedy Ann followed, giving children a new reason to love rag dolls and make their own versions.

Activity
Make a Rag Doll

Rag dolls of the 1800s are not easy to find anymore. They were so well "loved" over the years by children, and then their children and grandchildren, that they eventually fell apart. Even today, with factory-made dolls available at cheap prices, there is something special and lovable about a homemade rag doll.

MATERIALS

Pair of straight-edged scissors

Old T-shirt that can be cut up

Cotton balls

Needle and thread

Pencil

Scrap fabric

Fabric markers

All-purpose glue

Glitter, beads, sequins, or ribbon

Yarn

Cut two identical pieces of fabric from the T-shirt, each about eight inches high and roughly the shape of a bowling pin, only with a larger top (that will be the head). Place a few cotton balls between the two pieces, and sew the edges of the pieces together, almost all the way around. Leave about an inch open, and stuff more cotton balls inside until the body and head are as firm as you want. Use a pencil to poke the cotton into all corners of the doll's body. When the body is stuffed, sew up the hole.

Cut two sets of identical arm and leg pieces out of the T-shirt. These should each be about four inches long. Sew and stuff the arms and legs, as you did the doll's body. When they are finished, sew them to the body. Use some scrap fabric to make a dress for the doll and use fabric markers to draw on a face. Glue glitter and other decorative items onto the dress, and sew pieces of yarn to the head to make the doll's hair.

Chiseled, Carved, and Hammered

The essence of folk art is taking an ordinary object and having the creativity and vision to transform it into a charming piece of art. Sometimes that involves the use of paint or ink, or maybe a needle and thread. Other times, the art is made using a chisel, saw, or hammer. Wood and other raw material is carved, poked, chipped, etched, burned, or banged until it becomes a work of art.

All kinds of material can be carved and cut. Wood, bone, metal, and stone have all been used by folk artists to create treasured works of art.

Carved Furniture

Fine furniture was made by expert craftsmen who studied the art of furniture making. By the late 17th century, these expert "cabinetmakers," as they were known, were well established in North America. They helped furnish the houses of the wealthier classes of people.

But this expensive furniture was not the only alternative for people who wanted to sit on chairs and eat at tables. Many people fashioned their own furniture from available materials, or purchased it from local craftsmen who were not as expertly trained and did not have fine woods to work with. They created these pieces using their common sense, and sometimes their imagination. For example, while the Shakers (see page 86) made furniture that was very simple in appearance, the pieces were crafted in a style that was all their own. The Shakers are known for their ladderback chairs, which use many rungs to make up the back of the chair.

Many of these old homemade items are collected today as folk art because of their charm and beauty, whether simple or complex. Talent was required to make these pieces, even though they were not made by professionals. The intricately carved chair shown here is a perfect example of

**Chip-carved chair
by William Thorn Jr., 1892.**

Detail of chair.

the incredible level of achievement to which some of these often-unknown artisans soared.

Signed and dated pieces are rare, but this chair is inscribed in black ink on the bottom: "To Mrs. James Martha Maitland Thorn Fargis from her brother William Thorn Jr. and carved by him, 1892." Thorn created this masterpiece of woodworking by slowly chipping and carving away at the surface of two pieces of wood, one eight-sided and one four-sided. His design repeats several themes, including *fleurettes* (tiny, four-petaled, flowerlike symbols); 6-, 8-, 16-, and 18-pointed stars or rosettes with both straight and curved rays; and wafflelike grids (in the four corners of the seat). Crowning the seat's carving is a large central motif featuring what looks like a church's stained glass rose window, re-created in wood. The crowning whim of imagination of the chair is the

69

clover-shaped hole near the top, a touch that gives the chair extra depth. The entire edge of the chair seat and back is etched with an intricate border pattern. Do the patterns you see here remind you a little bit of Pennsylvania Dutch hex signs?

But unlike other folk art, folk furniture requires more than just artistic talent. Wood can be decorated and carved, but it must still be assembled into an attractive piece of furniture. In addition to creating all the delicate patterning, Thorn used his imagination several other times to create the chair. First, he chose not to make the seat a perfect, equal-sided octagon, like a stop sign, and the back not a perfect rectangle but a shape that is wider at the top than the bottom. Thorn was probably influenced by a European Gothic design he had seen. His beautiful design presented a problem, however—how could he attach the back of the chair to the base, or seat, of the chair?

There was only one solution, and it must have made him a little nervous. He had to cut the beautifully carved seat into two pieces, to allow him to make a rectangular hole into which to fasten the seat back. Carefully and slowly, Thorn sawed his seat. He knew that one mistake could mean disaster. When he was finished, he had to glue the seat back together, making sure the pieces lined up precisely. Thorn screwed two wooden braces on the bottom of the seat to make sure it would not crack in half. Thorn used his imagination once again to attach the finely turned legs to the bottom of the seat, creating a masterpiece of folk art. Considering the craftsmanship of this piece, chances are good that Thorn also carved other pieces.

While the chair is beautifully worked, part of its charm as a folk art wonder is that it is not completely symmetrical. Close examination reveals unevenness in the lines of the border, as well as some off-center patterns, but this is exactly what makes folk art furniture so endearing—it is not machine-made and it is not perfect. Hand-carved furniture is made by people with amazing abilities to see beauty in an ordinary piece of wood, plan out their ideas, and then create the piece without making any major errors.

Inlaid Wood

Carving is not the only way to create a folk-art masterpiece. Instead of carving a piece of wood to make an item of furniture, some people prefer the art of "marquetry," or the creation of inlaid wood. Marquetry is a little bit like quilting, except that wood is used instead of fabric. An artist begins with an undecorated piece of furniture, such as a chair or a table. Very thin strips of wood known as "veneer" are "inlaid," or precisely glued on top of the wood. The art of marquetry can be traced back to ancient Egypt and, later, to the Roman Empire. The invention of special saws eventually made it easier to cut pieces of wood that were precisely the same thickness.

Different types of wood can be used in a simple piece to create interesting contrasts in color and design. Some woods, such as birch, poplar, and pine, are naturally light. Some, such as mahogany, tulipwood, and red cedar, are pinkish red, while others, such as ebony, Indian rosewood, and African walnut, are naturally dark. Bone and ivory are also used. These have a pearly white color and rich creamy luster that cannot be found in wood.

Each type of wood has a different type of grain, the pattern of lines you see when you cut a piece of wood. Naturally occurring effects include lines that look like zebra stripes, wavy lines, called "tiger effect," and other three-dimensional-looking patterns that jump out at the eye. The folk art marquetry expert takes advantage of these different wood grains to complete the piece. The Shaker box shown on page 87 was made using inlaid wood.

A marquetry project is somewhat like a giant jigsaw puzzle, because the artist has to figure out what piece should go where. The most complicated marquetry furniture may have up to 20,000 separate pieces of inlaid wood.

Even furniture that is not inlaid with many little pieces of wood still uses many pieces of wood veneer. The fronts and tops of inexpensive pine and poplar chests and tables were often covered with beautiful mahogany veneers; making an entire chest out of mahogany would cost a fortune.

Canes and Walking Sticks

Back in the 19th century, most elderly or disabled people had to do their best to get around on their own. There were no nursing homes, and hospitals were uncommon, especially in rural areas. Arthritis medication and knee or hip replacement surgery did not yet exist, and wheelchairs were expensive. Workplace accidents were much more common

because working conditions were not always safe, and people whose legs were injured often never fully recovered. Canes and walking sticks were the only walking aids available to most people.

But the walking stick was also considered a fashionable accessory, and a young gentleman with no physical ailments might use one for an afternoon stroll with his sweetheart along the river's edge. The walking stick or cane was part of a well-dressed man's complete outfit, which included a suit and top hat or bowler (rounded) hat. The drawing of Joseph Collier on page 14 shows him carrying a walking stick.

Not every cane is considered folk art, but hand-carved ones definitely are. These were made in a stunning variety of intricately carved shapes, which included snakes, alligators, dogs, and other creatures. The cane shown on this page features the figure of a bearded man baring his teeth. While this cane is made of solid wood, others are made of wood and engraved or carved metal, bone, or ivory handles.

Gravestone Folk Art

Folk carving on gravestones can be traced back many hundreds of years. Stone was preferred over wood because it lasts much longer. Still, most of these ancient gravestones are long since crumbled, although a trip to old Irish graveyards may still reveal Celtic stones carved during medieval times.

Early American colonial gravestones of the late 17th century were fairly plain and simple. Those that were decorated usually featured a skull,

Walking stick, 1942.

or death's-head, carved into the tops of the stones. Often, a death's head had wings. Some skulls had two rows of bared teeth, while others had three rows. Each skull was different from the next, as each gravestone carver had a different style.

By the mid-1700s, Americans focused on a different aspect of death. Instead of the physical death of the body (represented by the skull), they were now more interested in the afterlife of the soul, and winged angel (also known as cherub) heads began appearing on gravestones. Whereas the death's heads were fairly simple in style, many cherubs featured hair, detailed smiling faces, and extravagantly designed wings. By the end of the 1700s, the cherub had replaced the death's head as the most popular stone decoration.

During this time, another design began to appear. Known as the "Urn and Willow" style, it was based on survivors' memories of the deceased, rather than on the dead person's body or spirit. The urn (a large vase) and willow (a tree associated with mourning) were classical symbols taken from ancient Greek and Roman times.

The illustrations shown here feature a death's-head from 1765 and a cherub from 1747. Stones like these can be found in the older cemeteries in cities and towns of the eastern United States, where the majority of Americans lived during the 1700s.

Decoys

Out on the calm waters of the inlet, a beautiful orange-billed, black-headed merganser duck floats peacefully by. The hunter raises his gun and takes aim. The duck does not see or hear the hunter and continues floating toward the shore. The hunter's finger is poised on the trigger, gently applying pressure for a split second, before he eases off and puts down the gun, sighing in frustration. He has just realized he was about to shoot a wooden decoy! So perfect was the "duck" that he almost could not tell the difference between it and the real thing.

Since the days of the first settlers, American hunters have tried to lure game birds, such as ducks and geese, out of the sky and into the water, within easy range of their guns. One way to do this is to use a decoy, in the hope that it will lure real birds to the water. The most common kind of decoy is made of wood and has glass eyes. It floats on the water's surface, bobbing up and down with the waves and sending a message to the real birds—"it's OK to come over here." Heads are sometimes "doweled," or fastened to the decoy's body with round pieces of wood called dowels, so that they can be turned to face any direction. There are dozens of varieties of game birds found in different parts of the country. Decoys of countless different species of ducks and geese have been made, including those of Canada geese, mallards, bluebills, pintails, redheads, eiders, canvasbacks, and goldeneyes. Female birds, or hens, look different from male birds, or "drakes," and different decoys are made for each.

Shorebirds are also popular subjects for decoy makers. These birds have long legs, and they stay near the coasts of lakes and oceans. They typically have long, pointed beaks. Shorebird

Death's head and cherub gravestone carvings, mid-18th century.

decoys have stilts for legs, which are stuck into the mucky marsh bottom or sandy beachfront. The decoy pictured here is probably that of a curlew, a type of shorebird with a slightly curved beak.

A successful decoy seems to have a life of its own. Of the thousands of decoys made, most were crude approximations of what a duck or bird should look like. A precious few decoys were made by talented carvers who had great artistic talent. These artists could breathe life into an otherwise dull piece of wood by tilting the bird's head or giving it a facial expression. By giving the decoy just the right body shape, colors, and overall appearance, an ordinary piece of wood was transformed into a masterpiece of folk art. Anthony Elmer Crowell (1862–1952) from East Harwich, Massachusetts, is considered the master of decoy making. The highest-quality bird decoys from the late 1800s and early 1900s are prized for their beauty, and today they may sell for up to many thousands each.

Old decoys are rarely found in perfect condition. Saltwater, moisture, and the alternating winter and summer temperatures have expanded and contracted the wood, causing cracks. Paint has been weathered, chipped, and faded by sunlight. Still, many people love to collect these folk art pieces.

Decoys of fish are also made, for the purpose of ice fishing in the northern areas of the United States. Unlike a duck decoy, a fish decoy is made to sink, not float. Hung from a string into a hole in the ice, the decoy is supposed to attract real fish, which the ice fisher attempts to spear. Fish decoys are made from wood, and they have a hollowed-out bottom that is filled with lead to make it sink.

Shorebird decoy, mid-20th century.

Tramp Art

The notch-carved wood pieces known as "tramp art" used to be considered junk. The name implied that the pieces were made by tramps, or hoboes, the early-20th-century terms for homeless people who traveled on trains from one place to the next, doing odd jobs. Tramp art has only recently been fully appreciated and welcomed as folk art. Only now do people realize that tramp art was not done only by tramps, but was a hobby for a variety of people. Older books on folk art do not even mention tramp art, but now pieces are found in museums.

The distinctive method used to make tramp art distinguishes it from any other kind of wood carving. In tramp art, thin strips of wood were notched or gauged to create a waffle effect. Especially common was edge notching, where the edge of a piece of wood was notched with a knife. The pieces of wood were then applied one on top of another with glue, or sometimes tiny nails, to create a rich, layered appearance. All tramp art has notching, and most tramp art is made from several layers.

Some pieces of tramp art were very crudely and unevenly done, while others were finely notched and elaborately designed. Like other forms of folk art, there does not seem to have been much in the way of written instruction for artists to follow. Tramp carving was probably passed on from one generation to the next or done by example—a piece done by one person inspired another person to create something similar. Tramp art is one of the most anonymous types of folk art, and

Tramp-art tray, early- to mid-20th century.

boxes, picture and mirror frames, clock housings, and small cabinets were especially popular tramp art items. Frames were common because they required little skill or talent to make, but looked impressive around a mirror or a picture.

The tray shown here is made of a 7½-inch-by-14-inch thin wooden base that was repeatedly gouged with a sharp metal instrument in a 10-pointed snowflake pattern. A second layer of notch-carved wood was then added around the edge as a border, along with a large wood rose on either side, and a center design that features a pheasant or bird of paradise on a branch. The bird feathers were made using the imprint of a U-shaped tool. The entire piece was then set into a dark-stained notched frame with glass, and notch-carved handles were attached to make a tramp art tray. The snowflakes were unevenly carved, and the central border around the bird is a little crooked. As with all kinds of folk art, tramp art is often raw and unique. Its imperfections are what give it character and distinguish it from machine-made items.

Tramp art is still made today, but the classic era of tramp carving is over.

Whittling, Carving, and Cutting

A distant cousin of tramp art is whittling. This hobby starts with a piece of wood, a pocketknife, and some spare time. Flakes of wood are whittled or peeled away with a careful flick of the wrist, and if the maker is inspired and talented enough, the end result will have some recognizable shape, such as that of a dog or a car.

most pieces are unsigned and undated, though we know that most pieces were created between 1900 and 1940.

As with much American folk art, the inspiration for tramp art came from Europe. Eighteenth- and 19th-century immigrants, especially from Germany, brought with them a love for woodworking. Chip carving was popular, but it required greater skill and more expensive materials. Notch, or tramp, carving was easier and cheaper. An overabundance of empty cigar boxes, which were made from soft, easily carved mahogany wood, during the late 19th and early 20th centuries meant that there was cheap and plentiful raw material available for craft projects. Anybody with a little spare time and a desire to work with wood could make something pretty. Jewelry or keepsake

different types of carving, including chip carving, notch carving, and others. Each artist uses the technique with which he or she is the most comfortable.

In addition to knives, artists use saws to cut wood into shapes. There are many different kinds of saws. In the 20th century, electric saws made wood cutting even easier. Each saw has its own application; some are good for cutting straight lines, some for curves. There are fine-toothed saws for delicate cutting work, and giant large-toothed saws for cutting huge pieces of wood. An electric saw can cut hard wood that might be difficult to carve. A saw can also allow an artist to make items more quickly, because it is faster to work with.

Millions of people across the country have woodworking shops in basements, attics, and garages. Since the first settlers came to America, countless hours of fun and hard work have been spent carving and cutting wood.

Models and Miniatures

To a child, nothing is more fascinating than seeing the world in miniature. Being able to take an entire world and shrink it down to a size that can be played with is magical, which is why many children never outgrow their love of models.

While folk art is sometimes described as primitive, three-dimensional folk art is often intricate, consisting of finely constructed models and sculptures. Models of ships, cars, and buildings have been made for many years. Each type of model is a specialty in itself and requires different skills. Wooden ships in bottles, for example, are made

Wooden sailor with signal flags, painted-wood calendar, 1945.

Wooden figure of a female baseball player, 1940s.

Woodcarving is a more refined version of whittling. Instead of flicking the wrist, the hand motion is more measured, and a carver probably wouldn't use a simple pocketknife. Many of the items shown in this chapter were carved. There are

75

Elijah Pierce

The African American minister and wood carver Elijah Pierce is one of America's most famous folk carvers. A religious man, he carved biblical and patriotic scenes in relief and then painted them in vivid colors. He believed that God's message was present in every piece he carved.

Born the son of an ex-slave, Pierce began carving when he was just a child. He carved little animal figurines from scrap wood, and he shared his work with anyone who admired it.

Pierce decided he wanted to become a barber, and that remained his profession for the rest of his life. After his first wife died at an early age, he traveled around the country in train cars for a while. His mother steered him toward religion, and he secured a preacher's license in 1920. He remarried in 1923. His second wife encouraged him to carve, and soon he was carving figures and setting them up in three-dimensional displays known as "dioramas."

His best work was the *Book of Wood* (1932), which told the story of Jesus in several panels of wood carvings. Over the years, he also carved nonreligious subjects including sports figures and other famous people, such as Abraham Lincoln.

Pierce finally received recognition from the folk art community in the 1970s. Exhibitions were organized, and he was written about in the *New York Times*. By the time he died in 1984, he was seen as the most respected and talented folk carver of the 20th century.

Figure of Abraham Lincoln by Elijah Pierce, carved and painted wood, circa 1975.

[1892-1984]

using a carefully designed system so that the folded-up ship can be erected with the pull of a string once the ship is in position inside the glass bottle.

Dollhouses, model houses, log cabins, and other buildings have been built by folk artists using scraps of wood, cardboard, metal, cloth, and a variety of miscellaneous decorative objects, including marbles, toothpicks, and acorns. An excellent example is a nearly eight-foot-high model of the Empire State Building. Made during the 1930s, it was constructed entirely of tiny wooden blocks that have been closely fitted together, using no nails or glue. This model is on exhibit in the American Folk Art Museum in New York City. Dollhouses, which are now purchased usually in toy shops, were once hand-made, along with miniature furniture, by fathers for their daughters.

Folk art dioramas are entire scenes that may include figures of people, animals, buildings, and vehicles. Elijah Pierce carved wooden figures and set them up to tell a three-dimensional story. One set of mid-20th century handmade dioramas recently put up for auction had an American western theme, and it featured figures of cowboys, bad guys, wagons, campfires, and horses. A good diorama implies movement, emotion, and tension, and is realistic enough to draw the viewer into the little world that the artist has created.

While paintings and drawings can take just a few hours, or sometimes even just a few minutes, to create, models require a lot more patience. What could possibly motivate model makers? Typically, the model maker has a deep love for the subject (for example, ship modelers tend to love the sea) or the material (many modelers simply love working with wood), and he or she has both the talent and the patience to see a project through to its completion—not an easy task, considering how many hours of tedious work it takes to construct a model from tiny parts that must fit together precisely. Advance planning is necessary to make sure that the end result is a success and that all the pieces will fit together to make an attractive whole.

Ships are some of the most commonly found folk art models. Made of wood that has been glued together and painted, many model ships are several feet long and must have taken their makers quite a long time to put together. Some model makers favor the more traditional sailing ships with their many masts and sails, while others were inspired by the technology of the late 19th- and early 20th-century steamships and ocean liners. Unlike today's model kits with detailed diagrams on how to assemble the pieces, the folk-art models are created from one's own knowledge and imagination.

Model making demonstrates American ingenuity, especially when the model itself is made to show a new invention. From its founding in 1790 up until 1880, the United States Patent Office required inventors to submit models of their ideas along with their patent applications. Thousands of models poured into the Patent Office. Eventually, fires and space shortages led the government to discontinue its model requirement, and the Patent Office wound up selling the models it had received to a private collector. After the collector died, the models were dispersed across the country. Although hundreds of thousands of patent models

Cardboard model of church, 1983.

were created, only a very small percentage of the inventions were ever manufactured at full size.

A patent was not the only reason a person might make a model. In the days before colorful brochures, computer presentations, and sales videos, people often relied upon models of the items they were trying to sell. This was especially true if the actual item was so large that a person could never travel with it. The "demonstration piece" used to sell this type of product was a hand-crafted model, with careful details and moving parts to show the potential buyer what to expect from the real thing.

Pyrography

Victorian folks tried almost anything to keep themselves entertained, which is why arts and crafts flourished during this time. Pyrography (Greek for "fire writing") was a popular hobby at the end of the 19th century, and it remained so until about 1940. For hundreds of years, pyrography had been accomplished mainly through the use of a hot poker or iron, and it was called "poker art." It was done by applying a red-hot poker to wood in order to engrave a design on the wood.

The Fleming Art Company was mainly responsible for the hobby's extreme popularity during the Victorian era and pyrography also became known as Flemish art. The company sold a complete kit, including a small and easy-to-use (compared to a red-hot poker!) benzene-fueled engraving tool. The company issued lavish catalogs that featured hundreds of different "blanks,"

The Little Town

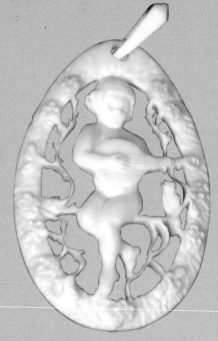

Ivory pendant carved in Erbach, Germany, by Willy Heilmann, late 20th century.

Seafaring men of the 1800s had easy access to whalebone, and so it is no surprise that bone carving, or "scrimshaw," was a popular hobby among them. Since prehistoric times, however, most bone carving occurred in places where ivory was available—in India and Africa, where elephants live. But what about an entire ivory carving industry springing up overnight in the middle of elephant-free Germany?

One day in the late 1700s, the young and adventurous Count Franz I of Erbach (1754–1823) returned from a trip to the southern reaches of Europe with a supply of *elfenbein* (German for elephant bone or ivory). On his journey, he had learned all about the art of ivory carving. Wouldn't it be great if people in the little economically depressed town of Erbach (about 30 miles southeast of the city Frankfurt) could learn to carve ivory just as he had on his travels? The pieces would certainly sell very well because they would be so rare and exotic, and perhaps the craft would even bring prestige and fortune to the town he loved.

The enterprising young count held a sample workshop in his home, the Erbach *Schloss* (castle), to demonstrate the art to the local horn carvers, who worked with deer antlers and wild boar horns. This precious new material appealed to the local carvers because of its purity and delicate white color.

In 1783 an ivory carving guild began in Erbach, and it was not long before the count's dream came true. By the mid-1800s, Erbach had become a world-famous ivory carving center. Young carvers served as apprentices to their elders, who were master carvers, and families passed the artistic traditions along from one generation to the next. Carvings ranged from tiny roses and animal figurines to large and complex sculptures and decorative pieces that took many months to create. Animals, including deer and wild boar, and the area's centuries-old tradition of hunting in the nearby Odenwald Forest inspired many designs. In this town, where the titles of "Count's Hunter and Forester" existed for hundreds of years, the forest was the most important source of folk traditions and folk stories.

Ivory carving in Erbach continued to grow in popularity, and during the second half of the 19th century the carvers produced many masterpieces. They worked in many styles, including classical Roman and Greek art and their own local folk-art style. In 1873, a carving known as the "Erbach rose" was awarded a medal at the Viennese World Exhibition. In 1892, a technical school for ivory carving and related trades was founded, making this profession even more popular.

Since the late 18th century, hundreds of immigrants to the United States have come from the Erbach area, bringing with them the traditions they grew up with in the Odenwald. Chances are that an Erbach immigrant or descendant picked up a piece of horn and carved something beautiful.

Today, Erbach has the only museum in the world that is dedicated solely to the art of ivory carving. The museum has over 2,000 carvings on permanent display, many of them created in Erbach. In the museum, local carvers give demonstrations of their art. Though the use of elephant ivory has been banned since 1989 because of dwindling elephant populations worldwide, the remaining ivory carvers in Erbach are happy enough to use the fossilized bone of ancient mammoths, whose 10,000-year-old remains are still found in the northern reaches of Russia. The streets along the main square of Erbach still have several shops that sell these carvings, a reminder of how, 200 years ago, a folk-art tradition breathed new life into the small town.

That Carved

or wooden items that were ready to be decorated. These wood bowls, glove boxes, napkin rings, plaques, and other decorative objects often had designs drawn on them so the user of the kit could follow the lines with the pyrography tool. Of course, it was also possible for a talented and creative artist to create pieces without using any guidelines. The Victorian-era kits were aimed at women, who were their main customers.

The engraving tool, which produced heat, but not a flame, worked best on softer wood, and the result was a brownish indentation about $1/16$ of an inch deep. Using the pyrography tool made by the Flemish Art Company and other companies, an artist could "draw" in a continuous line without stopping. The Flemish Art Company also made and sold a set of paints to be used on pyrography projects, as well as a punch set that allowed users to make holes in the wood and then glue glass gemstones into them. Common designs included fruit of all kinds, flowers (especially roses), horses, dogs, Native Americans, and well-dressed society ladies. One of the largest pyrography objects in existence is a wooden sign that is several feet long. It has a German version of the saying "There's no place like home" burned into it. The decorated bowl shown here is a more typical example and features cherries. It is marked "Flemish" (for the Flemish Art Company) on the bottom and is engraved by the hobbyist with a date of 1904 and the words "ZR to TR." Perhaps this was made as a gift from a wife to a husband, or vice versa.

Pyrography is still practiced today, though with different and more advanced tools than were available 100 years ago. New techniques include solar pyrography, which involves using a magnifying glass to concentrate the sun's rays onto wood.

Scrimshaw

Whaling was a profitable venture for 18th- and 19th-century Americans who lived in seaports along the Atlantic coast. Whaling parties were organized, and men set out on long voyages across vast oceans in search of great whales. The oil obtained from blubber, or whale fat, was burned in lamps, and whale meat and "baleen," giant plates of whalebone that whales used to strain plankton from the ocean bottom, were also prized.

Whaling ships traveled to different places, depending on the type of whale they were looking for. Ships had to head toward frigid Arctic waters in search of the 60-foot-long, 60-ton bowhead whale. In 1871, ice there trapped 32 ships. All the men escaped, but their ships were lost. The long and sometimes dangerous whaling trips provided the crew a lot of idle time. To fight boredom and keep their spirits up, nothing was better for the men aboard ship than to have something productive to do with their hands, and for many seafaring souls, scrimshaw was the answer.

Scrimshaw is the decorative carving or etching of animal teeth and bones. It was most popular in the United States during the 19th century, when whaling here reached its peak. Using tools such as a file, saw, awl, jackknife, and a sailing needle called a "pickwick," very beautiful objects could

Pyrography bowl with cherries, 1904.

The first step in making a scrimshaw from a whale tooth was to smooth the tooth with a piece of sharkskin or pumice, a very soft type of volcanic rock. A design could then be engraved onto the tooth, using the needle or other fine-pointed tool. Common designs included detailed pictures of the whaler's ship and the seaport from where he came. After the etching was finished, the engraving was inked. India ink, tobacco juice, wood ash, tea leaves, or vegetable dye were rubbed into the engraving so that the design would stand out. The final step was to buff the tooth to create a polished finished product.

In addition to teeth, whale bone was carved into a range of different objects. Sailing tools were a common form of carved object, and they ranged from sewing tools, such as thread spools, bodkins, which were used to make holes in fabric, thimbles, needle holders, and fabric clamps, to sailing tools such as fids, which were used to work with ropes, and sail seam rubbers, which were used to smooth out the creases in sails.

Of course, many other more decorative objects were also commonly made, including dominoes and other games, fine walking sticks, decorative boxes, and watch towers (elaborately carved stands used to house a man's pocket watch when it was not being worn). Some of these beautiful pieces were meant to be presents for sweethearts, who were waiting back home for the return of their loved ones.

Whaling ships also had another form of folk art affixed prominently to their bows—figureheads. These carved wooden figures were colorfully painted and were meant to bring good luck to the crew on their voyage.

Reproduction of a scrimshaw
on a whale tooth, 1870.

be created from the most readily available material—whale and walrus teeth and bones. Many fine etchings were done directly onto whale teeth. Their large size (about the size of a fist) and shape allowed a sailor to etch a fine design into both flat sides of the tooth. A young sailor on his first voyage would be taught how to carve by the more experienced crew members.

Activity

Make a Scrimshaw

Whaling was especially popular during the early to mid-19th century. One of the favorite pastimes of whaling captains and their crews, who spent months out at sea, was carving in whalebone, whale teeth, or walrus tusks, an art known as scrimshaw. In the actual scrimshaw process, a design is pricked onto the surface with a sharp knife or needle, and the holes are connected by delicate scratches. The engraving is then rubbed with ink and polished.

In this activity, you will make your own version of a scrimshaw.

MATERIALS

Adult to assist

Vegetable peeler

Small bar of Ivory soap

Pair of gardening or outdoor gloves

Fine black ballpoint pen

Using the vegetable peeler, whittle the soap into the shape of a whale tooth (roughly the shape of a tusk). Wear the gardening gloves while doing the carving, and always carve away from your body to avoid getting hurt.

Make your scrimshaw design by using the pen point to inscribe a picture of a ship on the flattest surface of the soap. If you'd like to, you can copy the ship seen in the illustration here. Make up a name for your ship, and carve that into the soap next to the picture of the ship. Carve the name of the "captain" of your ship. You can make scrolls or other designs on the other side of the soap.

How Do You Know if It Is American?

Many types of American folk art feature designs and symbols that originated in other countries. For example, Frakturs and hex signs often show themes that originated in Germany. Colorful birds and flowers are common in American folk art, but also in the art of many other countries.

So how do you know if a piece of folk art is *American* folk art? There are a few key questions to ask: Does the design look correct in style compared to known American pieces? Is the material commonly found in America? Is the form (the shape or type of item) of the object common in America? Does the object have a provenance, or ownership history in the United States?

Take a look at the picture of the engraved spoon shown here.

How was it made? The spoon appears to be some type of bone or horn that has been etched and then rubbed with a pigment to leave black color in the incised lines, the same method that sailors used to make scrimshaw. Many pieces of American folk art have been made using this method.

Design The spoon has many common design elements of Fraktur and scrimshaw, but the clothes of the man and woman—especially the man's hat—look exotic, not very American.

Bone spoon with engraved design, probably 19th century.

Since there is nothing sea-related on the entire spoon, chances are it was not made by a whaler.

Material and Form While carved powder horns and whale tusks are common in America, carved bone spoons are not so common. This makes it less likely to be American. It is also easier to identify an object if you have others to compare it to. A look at the folk art of other countries may reveal that somewhere in Europe, people favored making these decorative bone utensils. The bone could also be tested to see what kind of animal it came from, which may narrow the possible origins down.

Provenance Where was the item found? What is its ownership history? This information can be very valuable in determining its origins. Some love tokens and other pictures that look like American folk art were actually brought here by immigrants from Germany and other countries and passed down through the generations. In the case of the spoon, there is not much provenance available. The spoon, along with a matching fork, came from the estate of a New Jersey collector of utensils from the 18th and 19th centuries. The collector could have purchased the spoon anywhere.

So is the spoon definitely *not* American? It is very difficult to rule anything out, and there is always a slight chance, but the spoon is probably not American.

In 1975, the Endangered Species Act put an end to whaling by United States citizens, and thus severely limited the amount of scrimshaw that was done, although animal horns were still carved to create decorated powder horns that held gunpowder for old-fashioned guns of the 18th and 19th centuries. Today, folk artists continue to create scrimshaw using manmade materials.

Weather Vanes and Whirligigs

Today, if you want to know what the weather will be later, all you have to do is turn on the television or radio and listen to the weather report. But what did people do a hundred years ago? Why was knowing the weather even more important then than it is today?

Watching the weather was especially important in the countryside, where much of the population was engaged in farming or raising livestock. Crops depended on the right amount of rain to help them grow. If there was too little rain, seeds would not germinate, and plants would wither and die. If there was too much rain, seeds and plants would rot and become vulnerable to mold and fungus. If a farmer knew what was coming, he might be able to take measures to protect the crops.

Wind strength and direction could help a farmer tell if fair weather was going to prevail or if a storm was approaching. A lack of any wind told a farmer that the current weather front was going to hang around for a while. The direction from which a breeze is blowing can indicate that a warm front or a cold front is approaching. It can also indicate

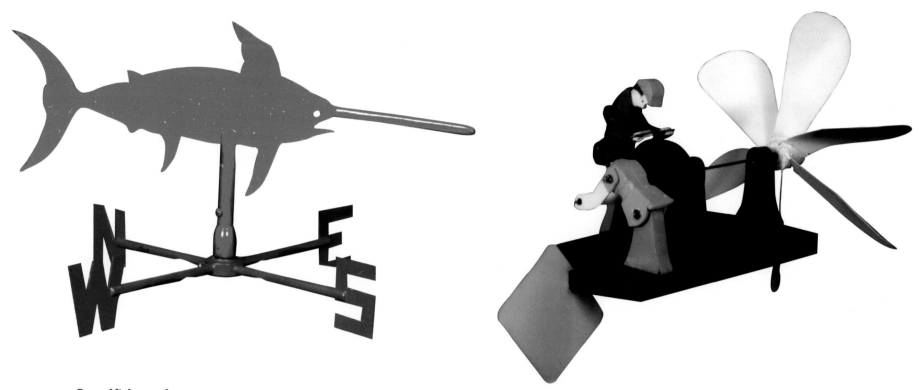

Swordfish weather vane made of metal, mid-20th century.

Whirligig by Peter Prommersberger, 1990.

if wet (low pressure) or dry (high pressure) weather is approaching. In the old days, the wind was about all a person had to help predict the weather.

Weather vanes were common in the 19th century, before the science of meteorology allowed for accurate reports of current weather conditions and predictions about the future weather. Weather vanes were created to stand atop farmhouses, where the wind could easily reach them. They were made from thin, durable material, such as sheet tin, iron, or copper, which could be easily blown by the wind without bending or breaking.

The softness and malleability of copper and tin allowed these materials to be hammered or shaped into attractive designs. A wooden model

was used as the basis for the design. From that, an iron mold was made for the metal to be hammered into. Copper weather vanes were often left unpainted so that they would turn green with exposure to the air. Some were gold-plated to make them more attractive and to protect them from decay. Wooden weather vanes were also made, but these did not hold up well over time because of decay.

Common weather vane designs included horses (with or without carriages or carts), roosters, Native Americans, angels, trains, ships, eagles, and arrows. Weather vanes were very popular from 1850 to 1920, but they continue to be made today, especially for use on older houses that have been restored to their former glory. The weather vane

Toy village with church and houses, mid-20th century.

Wooden giraffe with hinged legs, 1973.

Games and Toys

Although they had a lot of daily work to do, 19th-century people also had a lot of free time, especially during long, cold winters. Old-fashioned fun could be had playing games, but people had to make the game pieces themselves. By sawing a flat piece of wood into a square and applying a few colors of paint to it, a person could create a game board that would last generations.

Homemade game pieces ranged from plain, simple items to elaborately designed masterpieces of craftsmanship. The game of cribbage has been played for centuries, and handmade cribbage boards were common for hundreds of years. Many were quite intricate, and they often featured inlaid wood and bone marquetry.

Toys have been around almost as long as there have been children. An imaginative parent could fashion a few pieces of wood into a whole play village, or an ordinary stick into a carved animal. Before the days of the bicycle, a child might have had a homemade hobby horse (a carved wooden horse head attached to the end of a long stick) or rocking horse. Old-fashioned toys were simple and primitive, but kids loved them anyway. Most of the toys found in expensive toy shops could be nearly duplicated at home with some simple tools and a little hard work, and parents sometimes used toy making as a way to teach their children woodworking skills.

Today, antique toys are collected as folk art, but interesting or unique ones are difficult to find. As 19th-century children became adults and had

shown here was cut from sheet metal into the shape of a swordfish. The letters N, S, E, and W, which indicate north, south, east, and west, were also cut and soldered onto the weather vane's metal base.

Whirligigs were also designed to "catch" and move with the wind, but they were used more for decoration, not to tell the direction of the wind. Made of wood, whirligigs were originally given as toys to children. They ran with them, creating wind and moving the figures' paddle arms. Whirligigs are sometimes mounted onto a base, and some feature elaborate multi-part designs that move in different ways with the wind. The whirligig shown here features figures of a man and woman. When the wind blows, the man and woman turn a crank.

Make a Checkerboard

Checkers is a game that has been played in some form for thousands of years. It was imported to America from England, where a version called "draughts" is played. Its simplicity makes it a great game for kids, and strategy in its play keeps adults interested in the game. Homemade checkerboards are one of the easiest types of game boards to make.

MATERIALS

Ruler

Pencil

12-by-12-inch or larger square of wood, foam board, or cardboard

Red, black, blue, and white acrylic or poster paints

Small paintbrush

Stencil pattern of miniature stars or hearts

Stencil brush or small stencil sponge

Using the ruler, measure and mark a point 1 inch from each of the four edges of the game board. Draw a straight line in pencil that is parallel to the edge, so that you have a 1-inch border all around the board.

Measure the remaining width of the board. Divide that number by eight, and measure out the eight rows of squares. Draw a pencil mark at the top of the board, where each of the eight rows of squares will begin, and at the bottom where each row will end. Making sure your ruler is parallel to the edge of the board, connect the two corresponding pencil marks at the top and bottom of the board. Turn the board 90 degrees and repeat the process, so that you have a grid of 64 equal-sized squares drawn out in pencil.

Paint your checkerboard. Begin by painting the bottom left square black. Be careful to stay within the lines. Skip the next square and paint the third one black. Repeat this pattern across the bottom row, so that you have four black squares and four unpainted squares. Start the second row by painting the second square from the left black. Skip one and paint the next square black. Repeat this across the second row. For the third row, start at the left by painting the first square black. The pattern across the whole board should be that no black square is next to another black square.

When the black-painted squares have dried, paint the remaining squares red. Let the squares dry, then paint the border white. When the border is dry, use the blue paint, the stencil pattern, and the stencil brush or sponge to paint in the border. Repeat your stencil pattern around the entire edge.

The Shakers of

The sole surviving Shaker community is at Sabbathday Lake, Maine, where a few members still faithfully carry on the traditions started over 200 years ago by "Mother Ann," as founder Ann Lee is lovingly referred to. The community survived despite being one of the smallest and poorest of all the Shaker villages. There are currently 18 buildings on 1,800 acres of land. Members make baskets and small wooden items, and they package and sell home-grown herbs.

What does it mean to be a Shaker? What is Shaker life like? Do the remaining Shakers still make "worldly goods"? In the passage below, the Sabbathday Lake Shakers answer some questions about their lifestyle and their handicrafts.

"We are a very diverse group of people. Some members came in as children, grew up in the Community, and felt called to remain when they became adults. Others felt called by God to join as adults. What attracts us all is the life which calls us to live out our religion and calling every day.

"Our whole life is meant to be a continual prayer. When we rise in the morning, all say their private devotions. Immediately following breakfast, we have communal prayers at the table. These consist of responsive readings of two Psalms, two Bible readings, oral prayer, silent meditation, and finishes with the singing of a Shaker song. We all go off to our various chores and duties and meet again at 11:30 A.M. for a brief time of prayer. We dine at noon, go back to work until supper. On Wednesday evening we have Prayer Meeting. We also sometimes meet together for a singing meeting to learn songs or practice songs together. When we retire, we say

our prayers privately. On Sunday, we have the one service of the week which is open to the public, called Public Meeting. This starts with the reading of a Psalm followed by a Shaker hymn, then three readings from the Bible, another hymn, and then the Meeting is open to the moving of the Spirit. Any and all are invited to either offer a testimony [to speak before everyone] or join in singing. When the "gift" is out, then the Meeting is closed with a prayer and silent meditation. The guiding force in our life is our quest for God, and that is made most evident in our prayer life, just as it was for Mother Ann.

"We still make a variety of handcrafts here. We produce oval boxes [and] make knit, sewn, and woven items. We also make candy, jams, jellies, pickles, and relishes. We have an 1896 letter press on which we make cards, pamphlets, and limited-edition books. We all do some form of hand work following the injunction of our founder, Mother Ann: "Hands to work and hearts to God."

"We live with thousands of Shaker artifacts, so it is very difficult for anyone to pick out a single piece [that we like best]. For us, work is worship, and when someone produces something up to their full potential being, done in that spirit, then a piece stands out and has special meaning for all of us.

"Although it can be a little difficult to open a portion of our home to tourists, we feel it is an important tool to educate people on the history and beliefs of the Shakers. We also have many very fine objects that we are very pleased to be able to share with people who admire our handcrafts as well as our way of life."

Sabbathday Lake (1783–)

children of their own, they found that their kids preferred newer and "better" toys that were being made in factories. As a result, many of the old wooden toys that had been loved were discarded. That might explain the rarity of 18th- and 19th-century toys in existence today. Although many children today have never played with a hand-made wooden toy, in parts of Europe (especially Germany, which is known for its toy-making heritage), handmade toys are still carved and painted by the thousands every year for eager children.

Shaker Arts and Crafts

The Shakers began in England in 1758 as an off-shoot of the Quakers. Known as the United Society of Believers in Christ's Second Appearing, they were led by a woman named Ann Lee. Their original name was the Shaking Quakers, because of the shaking movements of the dance that was incorporated into some of their prayer ceremonies. Ann Lee immigrated to America in 1774, bringing the Shaker movement with her, and settled near Albany, New York, where there is now a boulevard called Albany Shaker Road in their honor. The first distinct Shaker village was founded in New Lebanon, New York, in 1787. The community of 500 people had several buildings devoted to making items to be sold, including an Extract House, where herbs and flowers were crushed and essential oils, including dandelion and butternut, were extracted; a Seed House; and an Herb House, which handled 70 tons of herbs per year; and workshops, in which furniture was made.

Shaker "Poland Spring" box, made by the Sabbathday Lake Shaker Community, late 19th century.

The religion spread to other states, including Maine, Massachusetts, Connecticut, New Hampshire, Kentucky, Indiana, and Ohio. At its peak during the 1830s and 1840s, there were as many as 5,000 to 6,000 members of the Shaker organization. But the Shaker movement was not destined to last, partly because the religion did not allow marriage, and therefore the Shakers did not have children of their own. They did take in orphaned children and raised them as Shakers, but that was not enough to keep the Shakers going as the 20th century progressed.

A life of simplicity and hard work was one of the most important features of Shaker society. The following traditional Shaker hymn is very well known. The expression and feelings in Shaker art are perfectly mirrored here:

> 'Tis the gift to be simple, 'tis the gift to be free,
> 'tis the gift to come down where we ought to be
> and when we find ourselves in the place just right
> 'twill be in the valley of love and delight.
>
> When true simplicity is gained
> to bow or to bend we shan't be ashamed;
> to turn, turn shall be our delight
> till by turning, turning we come 'round right.

Because of their dedication to being self-sufficient, the Shakers made almost everything they used, from nails to their own furniture, and they grew their own crops as well. The baskets, boxes, chairs, rugs, and quilts that they made by hand are now treasured as folk art. The chairs they made, known as ladderback chairs, have seats woven out of cane or textile tape. Shaker-made oval boxes are unique; they were made with thin wood that was formed into an oval shape and held together with finger-like splints and copper tacks as fasteners.

Shakers were not completely isolated from modern life. They recognized that they had to sell some of their handicrafts and products to pay for expenses. The items they sold to the general public were known as "worldly goods," and they are collected as folk art today, just as the items the Shakers made for their own use. The so-called "Poland Spring" box shown here was sold by the Sabbathday Lake Shaker Community in Maine. It was made to be kept on a dresser and used for the storage of jewelry and other small valuables. Made with inlaid wood, these handsome, yet simple, boxes exemplify the Shaker philosophy.

Order and cleanliness were important to the Shakers, and this was reflected in their villages and in their crafts. The Shakers placed importance on education, and they embraced technology and science to help them produce the highest-quality products and to work in the most efficient manner. As an 1859 book on life along the Hudson River stated about the New Lebanon, New York, Shakers: "All are willing, diligent, and faithful workers, and all appear to be cheerful, comfortable, and happy. The articles they manufacture stand deservedly high in public estimation [esteem], the very term 'Shaker' being a sort of guarantee that the article is genuine."

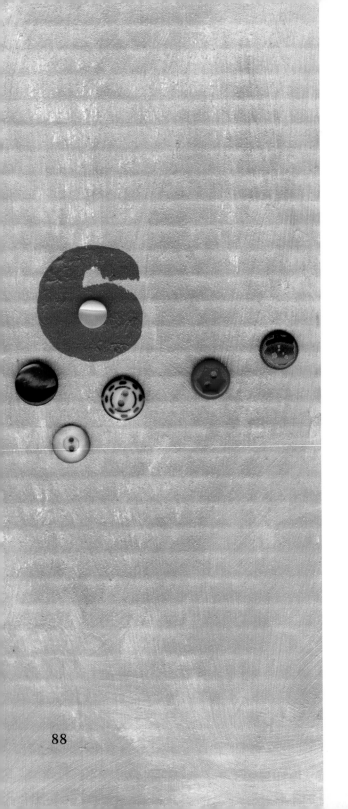

Found Objects and Scraps

Folk art proves the saying, "One person's junk is another person's treasure." Folk artists are happy to experiment with and use many different types of materials and media to create their art. Old scraps and discarded junk are commonly recycled and made into objects of art by folk artists all around the world. In fact, some folk artists use *only* scrap materials and junk, also called "found objects." Found objects can be discovered in many places: at flea markets, junkyards, and garbage dumps; in the woods; buried

Clothespin chair, mid- to late 20th century.

in the ground; on the beach; on streets and sidewalks; in attics and basements; and even in a pocket. Some artists focus on one type of object, such as bottle caps. Others collect a wide variety of materials for their use.

When the Industrial Revolution hit full steam around 1850, reliance on handmade objects decreased, and machine-made (manufactured) items became commonplace. What had been produced by hand in limited quantities was now being made by machine in mass quantities. Everything from glass bottles to metal buttons and nails was readily available to the general public at affordable prices. The millions of mass-produced, disposable items became the source of cheap found objects for use in artworks.

With these found objects, folk artists make sculptures, clothes, collages, and other pieces of art. Though folk artists have been using scrap materials for hundreds of years, collage in particular became very popular when artists such as Picasso and Georges Braque used train tickets, feathers, cloth, hair, and other found objects in their paintings. The German artist Max Ernst and others who belonged to a 1920s art movement called "dadaism" used discarded items to create miniature three-dimensional rooms and scenes. More recently, pop artists Robert Rauschenberg and Jasper Johns have used tennis

balls, coffee cans, and clocks, among other items, in their artworks. These works have been called "shadow boxes," "assemblages," "collages," and "mixed media" (meaning that the art is made of different types of materials). One of Rauschenberg's most famous "combines" (as he called them) contained a stuffed goat, a police barrier, a tire, a tennis ball, and part of a shoe.

In this chapter, we will look at all kinds of found, rescued, and recycled objects, including scrap wood, buttons, and bottlecaps.

Different people have access to different types of scrap objects. Electricians have spare wire and switches. Tailors, seamstresses, and dressmakers often have extra buttons and ribbon. Watchmakers are able to get plenty of watch parts. Plumbers usually have extra pipes and washers, and carpenters have plenty of scrap wood. There are plenty of places where anyone can find objects and scrap materials to use in folk art. Someone living in the city might have access to lots of bottles, cans, and bottle caps. Someone living near a lumberyard would have access to scrap wood, while someone living near a junkyard would easily find old car parts. A hardware store has plenty of nails and screws. Flea markets and garage sales also provide opportunities to find many inexpensive materials.

Before the 20th century, there was no garbage collection service. Instead, people buried their junk and garbage in a dump or a trash pit. Only during the 20th century did people begin to put

89

Activity
Create a Memory Box

During the late 19th and early 20th centuries, found objects and assorted keepsakes were often worked into clay lamp bases or jugs, or glued to wooden boxes. The resulting "memory jug" or "memory box" featured bits and pieces of the person's life, such as medals, ticket stubs, buttons, coins, and photos—saved and found scraps that had some meaning to the person who made it.

Here you will make a memory box that you can use to preserve bits and pieces of your life, as well as to store money, jewelry, or other items. Just be sure not to decorate it with anything so valuable or meaningful that you will regret gluing it onto the box!

MATERIALS

Any assortment of small items that have meaning for you. Possible items include shells found on the beach, marbles, pieces of broken jewelry, buttons, coins, rocks, baseball cards, movie ticket stubs, dried flowers, toy soldiers, pictures of friends, and key chains.

Strong glue or epoxy

Hinged, unfinished wooden box (available at a craft store)

Ask a parent for permission to use the glue. Arrange and glue your found items and memorabilia onto the top and sides of the box so that it is completely covered. Allow the glue to dry thoroughly before using the box.

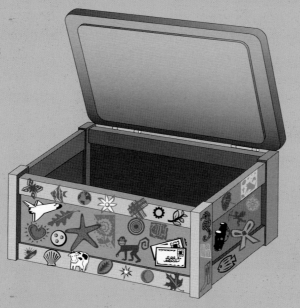

Box made from coffee stirrers, 1979.

trash out at the curbside for pick up. Suddenly, the things that people put out for garbage were available as raw materials for junk collectors and artists. Everything from coat racks and tables to teapots and picture frames is piled neatly on the curb, waiting to be hauled away by a garbage truck or rescued for use in a project. Because of recycling programs, glass and metal items are now often separated from the rest of the trash, making it even easier for the users of found objects to find what they need. It is best to leave salvaging garbage to the professionals because items that are thrown away may have sharp edges, and objects can be dirty and may need to be washed or sanitized.

A Houston, Texas, man named Cleveland Turner has collected junk for years. He has transformed the outside of his home into a display of found objects of all kinds. Stories such as this can be found all across the country; wherever there is

Recycled Fun

Many common recyclable items are thrown out every week. Examples of these items are toilet paper tubes and paper towel tubes, milk jugs, bottle caps, plastic film containers, and buttons. What kind of outdoor collage or sculpture could a folk artist make using a few of these items, some glue, and some imagination?

Tin man, 1994.

junk, there are people who find new and interesting ways to transform it into art.

Found objects inspire everyday people to create folk art. Making these funny sculptures and creations can become an addictive hobby. Some artists sell their creations to make a little extra money on the side. One man in New York could often be seen selling his wind toys from his car in a supermarket parking lot. The tin man shown here was found for sale on a front porch near Liberal, Kansas. It was made by a woman in a rural area not far from the place where the Yellow Brick Road Festival (celebrating *The Wizard of Oz*) is held each year.

The beauty of found objects is like the beauty of folk art itself—there are no rules. What an artist does with the raw material is up to him or her, and anything goes. Gregory Warmack, an artist who goes by the nickname Mr. Imagination, is famous for his bottle-cap figures and other artworks made with found objects, including buttons, feather dusters, industrial sandstone, and old paint brushes. The bottle caps make good raw material because they come in so many colors and designs.

Even unlikely junk can become art. The American Folk Art Museum has a small rug made only of small pieces of red, white, and blue plastic Wonder Bread bags.

For an imaginative folk artist, finding objects to use is as easy as grabbing some pocket change. The photo on page 93 shows a clock that was made recently using a collection of old coins. Included are buffalo nickels (made until 1938), Mercury dimes (made until 1945), and wheat

91

Mr. Imagination

Self-Portrait
by Mr. Imagination, 2003.

[b.1948]

Since he was a little kid growing up in a large family in Chicago, Gregory Warmack was an artist. He used pieces of cardboard boxes and his imagination to create art. He painted the cardboard with old paintbrushes. When the brushes were no longer usable, he cut a twig from a tree and used the rough end as a brush. As an adult, he did a variety of jobs to help pay the bills, including working in restaurants waiting tables and washing dishes. He also made and sold his own jewelry. Warmack got his first recognition in early 1978, when a local newspaper ran a story about the intriguing man who sold his wares at their offices.

Then one summer day not long after the article appeared, Warmack nearly died after being robbed and shot twice in the stomach just a few blocks from his apartment. He lay in a coma for a month and a half. When he finally awoke, he had to learn to walk and write again. He discovered that his passion for making art had increased. "I was always an artist; I just got more in tune. I was able to see more," he says.

One of his favorite materials was a sandy stone that he saw being dumped by a truck. When he tried to carve his initials in the stone, he discovered that the stone was made of a soft material that was very easy to work with. His tool of choice became a nail. He also noticed that as he carved, sand fell from the stone. He used the loose sand to make sand paintings. A couple of years after being injured, Warmack adopted the name Mr. Imagination.

Mr. Imagination believes he may have journeyed back into the past, to ancient civilizations, while he was in the coma. "When I pick up a piece of stone and start to carve, I see ancient faces," he explains. He works by candlelight because "it helps bring out the spirit in the stone." In addition to sandstone, Mr. Imagination uses old paintbrushes, feather dusters, broom heads, buttons, and bottle caps in his art. He is fascinated by bottle caps—one cap may not look like much, but put a bunch of them together and the result is a "shine that makes it magical." He has made several glorious bottle-cap thrones by blanketing ordinary chairs with bottle caps. He has also created numerous bottle cap staffs and figures, both human and animal. And he never goes anywhere without his trademark bottle-cap hat, which is well worn from all his travels and from all the handling by the people he lets try it on.

He is enthusiastic about using recycled materials. About bottle caps, he says "I feel I am preserving part of history. One day there aren't going to be any more caps. One day when I'm gone off this earth, people will say, 'Wow! Bottlecaps!' "

Mr. Imagination was first "discovered" by the art world in 1983, when a gallery began showing his works. He developed a following among people who were interested in self-taught and visionary art. Though some people refer to him as an "outsider," he does not like that term very much. He has been commissioned to design sculptures for the House of Blues restaurant chain, as well as for the 1996 Olympics in Atlanta. Now, even though he is famous and his art is in the collections of the Smithsonian Institution and the American Folk Art Museum, Mr. Imagination insists that success has not changed him. He still lives for his art, and for teaching kids how to use their imagination by showing them that almost any "trash" object can become an integral part of a dazzling artwork.

Mr. I, as his friends call him, is not only a prolific artist, but also a collector. He estimates he has 20,000 to 30,000 pieces of art, his own and others'. He also collects toys and antiques. His apartment is cluttered with the fruits of his creative mind. Though he has moved from his native Illinois to Pennsylvania, people in Chicago still send him bottle caps that they have saved. He keeps a supply of industrial sandstone in storage for future use.

Mr. I is now experimenting with new technology as a way to create alternate versions of his art. With the help of fellow artists, Mr. I has created virtual sculptures, or three-dimensional images drawn on the computer. His experimentation shows how the future of folk art could be filled with wonderful surprises.

pennies (made until 1958). An Illinois artist surrounded a picture of President Lincoln with a frame of several rows of shiny pennies, and on the back of the art wrote, "Made with gold pennies." Coin collages are fun and easy to make.

Shadow boxes are another good way to use found objects. A three-dimensional frame or open box is used as the base in which to arrange and glue various found objects to make a little self-contained world that can be hung like a regular picture. Though he was not a folk artist, Joseph Cornell (1903–1972) was famous for his fantastic shadow boxes that were full of interesting clippings and objects.

These days, not all "found" objects actually need to be found or salvaged. The existence of crafts stores makes it easy for an average person to obtain a large number of popsicle sticks, pipe cleaners, small wooden blocks, and other items for use in a collage or model. As mentioned earlier, people whose jobs deal with small parts are likely to have access to extra pieces. A retired watchmaker who realized that he had hundreds of tiny spare watch parts used them to make a collage picture of an old Chevrolet car.

Coin-collage clock, 2003.

Lincoln penny frame by T. Peeples, 1978.

Trench Art

Humans have a tendency to take even the worst situations and make something good out of them. During the treacherous days of World War I (1914–1918), with bullets and shells flying and poison gas wafting through the air, soldiers were eager to find something to take their minds off the horror of war. Making art was a way to keep their hands and minds occupied in the midst of a terrible conflict. Trench art was named for the trench-

Where Can Folk Art Be Found?

Creating folk art pieces can be fun, but what if someone wants to collect folk art? Where are the best places to look for folk art? It is best if an adult is involved in the search, to help you determine what is trash and what is treasure. Here are some helpful tips:

1) Visit local garage sales, yard sales, and house sales. Older sellers may have accumulated some interesting items, including samplers, handmade knickknacks, hex signs bought in Pennsylvania Dutch country, hand-painted dishes or decorative ceramics, stoneware, primitive paintings (sometimes done by the seller), whirligigs, art made with found objects, and wood carvings.

2) Explore thrift and consignment shops. These stores are sometimes run by a local church or charity, which uses the profits made from sales to help persons in need. All kinds of odds and ends can be found in a thrift shop.

3) Try a flea market. This is the name given to an organized gathering of merchants selling new and used items. Flea markets are often held in parking lots.

4) Check out a local antiques shop. These stores often have nice pieces of folk art.

5) Remember that most items are sold "as is," with all their flaws, chips, cracks, and sometimes questionable authenticity.

Trench-art vase made from World War I shell, 1918 or 1919.

Hex sign by Zook, found at a garage sale, mid 20th century.

spent in trenches were both dangerous and at times quite boring.

Metal is to a soldier what whalebone was to a 19th century sailor—the most widely available material. During the height of World War I, millions of shells were fired. An exploded shell created

Activity

Make a Gum-Wrapper Chain

Ordinary objects can be used to create something artistic. For example, gum wrappers can be recycled into links that can then be made into a chain. These chains can then be used as the basis of other works of art. In this activity, you will make a gum-wrapper chain of your own.

MATERIALS

15 to 50 paper gum wrappers from stick chewing gum

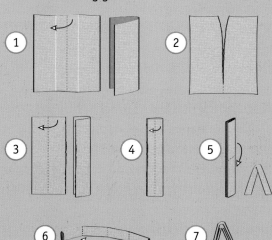

To join links:

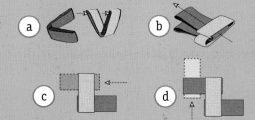

Peel open one gum wrapper at its seam. Fold the paper crisply in half lengthwise, and gently and neatly tear the paper in half along the crease. (If you prefer, you can cut the paper using scissors.) Now you have 2 links for your chain.

Fold one of the links in half lengthwise, then in half lengthwise again. Flatten the folds with your fingertips. Fold the strip in half to make a center fold, then open the strip and fold the top and bottom in toward the center fold; the ends should be tucked into the middle. Repeat with the other gum wrapper halves.

Join the links. Hold one link in your left hand, with the folded edges facing you. Take another link in your right hand, with the folded edges facing you. Push the ends of the piece on the right inside the folded pieces of the piece on the left and pull tightly. Continue joining the links, forming a zigzag chain. If you have a variety of wrapper colors you can create a pattern, or you can just randomly link them. You can use the chain as a necklace or to decorate something. For example, you could glue a chain along each edge of a picture frame.

Gum-wrapper chain, 1980s.

95

Activity
Button Collage

Buttons are popular items for making folk-art pictures and sculptures because they are pretty and colorful, affordable, durable, and easy to find. One giant picture made entirely of buttons was recently for sale at a folk art gallery. Buttons come in many materials, including plastic, glass, wood, ceramic, stone, and shell. They have been used for hundreds of years for everything from shirts and sweaters to pants and coats. In this activity, you will use them to make a collage.

MATERIALS

Several sheets of 8½-by-11-inch card-stock paper, or several 3-by-5-inch index cards

At least 100 buttons of several different sizes and colors

All-purpose glue

There are no rules for this activity. To make a two-dimensional picture, use the paper as a base upon which to glue the buttons. Arrange the buttons any way you like. You can create a picture of an object, make a smiley face, or write your name or birth date. One way to accomplish this is to apply swirls of glue to the whole area of the paper, then place buttons onto it in some kind of design or pattern.

You can also make a sculpture with the buttons by gluing them to each other to make the figure of a man, a dog, or anything else you like.

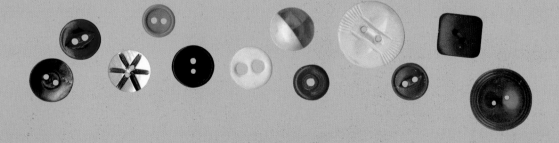

spent in trenches were both dangerous and at times quite boring.

Metal is to a soldier what whalebone was to a 19th century sailor—the most widely available material. During the height of World War I, millions of shells were fired. An exploded shell created "shrapnel," or fragments of metal. The shrapnel, along with whole, unexploded shells, was often just a few feet away from the soldiers. The copper shell casings were very malleable (soft and pliable) and could be hammered or bent to create designs. Soldiers used these plentiful materials to create small works of art, keepsakes of their time on the battlefield. These ranged from souvenir letter openers to vases, lamps, and ashtrays.

Another variety of trench art was created by civilians after the war, as keepsakes for the relatives who visited the battlefield where their loved ones perished. A copper letter opener made from a shell casing was inscribed "Somme Souvenir 1919." It may have been made by a soldier after the war ended, or by an enterprising civilian who sold it to a tourist or a battlefield pilgrim. The Somme was a region of France along the English Channel that saw heavy fighting during World War I.

Similar to trench art is:

Prisoner-of-war (POW) art. This consisted of knickknacks, paintings, and drawings made by many of the millions of prisoners of war who were captured and held for several months or even years, especially during World War II. One former German World War II POW donated all 315 of

Make a Bottle-Cap Figure

During the past 100 years, folk artists have used the disposable products of the machine age. These items are manufactured by the millions, and it is very easy to accumulate a large supply of them. Some people who grew up during hard times are now very thrifty, and they collect and save many things. Others just enjoy having a lot of "stuff" around.

Metal bottle caps were first made in the 1890s. Before long, everyone from folk artists to Boy Scouts were collecting used bottle caps. One man collected more than 500,000 bottle caps and decorated his restaurant and bar with them. Mr. Imagination takes his bottle cap–covered hat wherever he goes.

Using wooden blocks for the head and torso and bottle caps for the arms and legs, some artists have created unique works of folk art. Now it is time to make your own bottle-cap figure. Remember to use your

MATERIALS

Small pair of pliers

50 to 75 ruffle-edged bottle caps (see note)

All-purpose glue

Wooden cube, about 1 inch on each side (from hobby store)

Wooden block, about 2 inches square and 1 inch thick

Flat wooden base, about 4 by 4 inches

Empty 12-ounce soda can (optional)

2 to 8 tiny (¼-inch diameter) buttons

Acrylic paints, various colors (optional)

Paintbrush (optional)

Use the pliers to straighten out any dents in the caps.

Glue together 12 to 18 bottle caps, one on top of another, in order to make a straight arm or leg. If you want the arm to be bent, glue together 6 to 9 caps, and then glue together another string of 6 to 9 caps. Let the glue dry, then glue the "upper" and "lower" arm pieces together at whatever angle you want. Use the blocks for the head and body of a human figure (or the soda can for the body of an animal), and glue your arms and legs in place. Decorate the figure, using the tiny buttons for eyes and to represent actual clothing buttons on the figure's body. If you like, you can also paint the figure.

Note: If you can't find enough of this type of bottle cap, you can also use the larger, flat metal twist off bottle caps, or even ¾-inch- to 1-inch-diameter buttons instead.

A Gift of Folk Art

Some folk art is made strictly for personal use and enjoyment, and is never really intended for the outside world to see. Other works of folk art are made to be presented to friends or family as gifts or awards. For example, sailors' valentines often are made with shells collected overseas and meant for a sweetheart back home.

The model pipe organ shown here is made of wood blocks and 90 pieces of wood dowel. In fading black letters along the tops of the second largest set of pipes reads the word "Congratulation," and the little piece of sheet music placed atop the keyboard is titled "Old 100th". The entire organ was originally painted the same brown color as the base, but it looks like someone later spray painted the pipes gold and added the little plastic keyboard.

Perhaps this was a gift for someone's 100th birthday, perhaps someone named G. Taylor who used to play the organ. Many gift folk art items will always remain a mystery, because they were meant to have a private meaning that only a few people in the world would understand. This air of mystery intrigues collectors and attracts them to folk-art items that were made as gifts. Because they were made with such love and care, folk art gift pieces are usually exquisitely intricate and beautiful.

his works to the Thunder Bay Military Museum near the site where he was held at a camp in Monteith, Ontario, Canada. Prisoner-of-war art dates back well before World War II. Even during the War of 1812, French prisoners of the British were carving works of art out of bone.

Prison art. Beautiful boxes made of matches and other handcrafted objects have been made by men and women who are locked in prison.

Decoupage bowl, late 19th century.

G. Taylor's Organ, early 20th century.

Activity

Decoupage a Box

The word "decoupage" is from the French word decouper, *meaning "to cut out." Although it had been practiced for centuries, the popularity of this activity soared during Victorian times. Some commonly decoupaged items of that era include bowls and boxes, which were covered with cigar bands, pieces of wallpaper, and other paper cutouts. The creative freedom of decoupage is what makes it so enjoyable: you can choose and cut out any interesting bits of paper and paste them down in any fashion that appeals to you.*

Round boxes called hat boxes or band boxes were used to store hats and other personal travel items during the 19th century. In this activity, you will decoupage your own round box.

MATERIALS

Pair of scissors

Wrapping paper, newspaper, wallpaper, or pages from a favorite magazine; use pictures of cars for example, to make a storage box for Matchbox cars, or pictures of jewelry to make a jewelry box

Decoupage glue (available at craft stores; try to find one that is glue, sealer, and finish all in one)

Round box with a lid

Paintbrush

Clear varnish (if the decoupage glue is not all-in-one)

Cut the paper into small (2 to 4-inch) squares. Glue them to the box and lid at different angles, so that they overlap one another. Be careful not to use too much glue, or the paper will not lay flat.

If you don't have the all-in-one glue, apply two coats of varnish to the outside for a smooth finish. If the all-in-one type is used, brush it over the top of the glued pieces as well. Your finished product will be an interesting collage of colors and patterns.

Public Folk Art

Some of the best folk art was not really intended to be art at all. Its creators certainly had no idea they were making anything that would be preserved many years later. Public folk art was created to be seen by the masses, exposed to the elements, touched, and used.

The signs, advertisements, and patriotic art that were common over 100 years ago are now valued by collectors, and also by historians, for what they can tell us about our society. Lovers of folk

art treasure the humor, the bright colors, and the fancy decorative lettering of early advertising. Though in some cases it may have been mass-produced, this early advertising was much closer to folk art than academic art because it was the art of the common person. Nineteenth-century public folk art is certainly a far cry from the slick multi-billion-dollar advertising industry of today.

Product Design

Nationally known brand names were very rare until the 19th century. Prior to the 1900s, hand-made products were created in limited quantities, and they were distributed on a local scale. In the 19th century, however, mass production and the invention of the railroad allowed companies to send their products across thousands of miles. Suddenly, people had a wide variety of products they could choose from. Should they buy soap that was made by the Royal Soap Company, or soap made by the Imperial Soap Company?

The appearance of the product's packaging became important. Products were displayed next to rival brands, and a more interesting box meant a better chance of selling the item. Some of the most folksy packages of the 1800s are the ones that contain products that seem rare or exotic today.

Trade Cards and Color Advertising

Product packaging alone was not enough to sell mass quantities of an item, and merchants could no longer rely just on word of mouth to sell their products. During the 19th century, public announcements were created to reach a much wider audience.

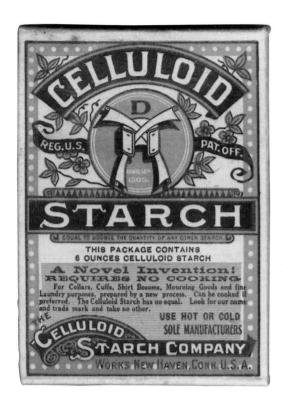

Front of Celluloid Starch box, circa 1905.

Trade card collage, 1880s.

Activity
Design a Shaker Seed Packet

As you have read, the Shakers were a relatively small group of several thousand people who lived in various communities in the eastern United States during the 19th century. Shaker design and art remain popular today.

One innovation made popular by the Shakers was the use of individual envelopes to package and sell seeds. Before that, seeds were sold by the pound and were measured out of large glass containers. The Shakers designed colorful display boxes, as well as the individual seed packets to place in them for display. This folk art was an early precursor to modern advertising—the Shakers used pretty designs and colors to get people to buy something.

In this activity you will make a few Shaker-style seed packets.

MATERIALS

Knife (adult supervision required)

Two large white grapefruits

Two large pink grapefruits

2 paper towels

Magic markers of various colors

Several 2-by-4-inch or 3-by-5-inch white and yellow envelopes (the kind with the flap on the short end)

Poster or tempera paints of various colors

Fine paintbrush

Cut the grapefruits in half. Take out the largest seeds; these are the ones that can germinate. Place the seeds from the pink grapefruits on one paper towel. Using a magic marker, write "pink" on the towel. Place the seeds from the white grapefruits on the other towel, and write "white" on the towel. Set the labeled seeds aside to dry in a cool, dry place for a couple of days.

Decorate the envelopes with pictures of grapefruit and other colorful designs that you wish to include. Draw or paint the words "Pink grapefruit seeds" on half of the envelopes, and "White grapefruit seeds" on the others. Write in a price of "2 cents" on each envelope.

When the seeds are completely dried you can put them into the proper envelopes and seal them. You can give them to friends as gifts. Tell them to plant the seeds in a 6-inch-diameter pot. In a week or two, the seeds should sprout into decorative grapefruit plants!

Some of the first advertisements appeared in newspapers, and they were usually for cold or other sickness remedies or self-improvement products. Though they sometimes included illustrations, most early ads relied heavily on words, which explained, in long, drawn-out stories, why a product was good. Advertising evolved during the mid-to-late 19th century with the introduction of trade cards. Companies designed small cards, with beautiful pictures on the front and highlights of their product on the back, in order to help sway people to buy their product. The cards were given out at local shops. These trade cards had a primitive innocence, and sometimes a humorous quality, to them. The idea was to awe the consumer with beautiful pictures, not with a lot of writing. Some trade cards featured a picture of a smiling character holding the product, while other cards had just a pretty picture. Babies and children were often depicted in various poses, including playing instruments, riding bicycles, playing games, in scenes from popular stories, or riding on large dogs or birds.

The ads were supposed to be comforting reminders of the pleasant things in life (just as folk-art primitive paintings showed happy everyday scenes). Companies wanted to show that their product was just right for the average person— "It is not too good; just good enough" to quote an 1885 advertisement for Star soap. The introduction of the color printing process in the 1870s made it easy and cheap to produce full-color trading cards. Even popular figures such as Santa Claus were called into service to advertise for various

Wooden cigar-store Indian
by Samuel Robb, late 1800s.

brand names, beginning a long advertising tradition of celebrity "endorsements."

Some trade cards were rectangular, and others were "die-cut" (machine-stamped out into special shapes), such as those of angels or plants. Made by the thousands, these bright and colorful cards quickly became collector's items, and Victorian girls raced home from the market to glue their new trade cards into beautifully bound souvenir books with blank pages, called scrapbooks. It was a creative challenge to arrange the different cards on each page of their scrapbooks. These old scrapbooks are prized today. Collectors soak the brittle old paper to dissolve the glue, and then remove the trading cards. The rapidly disappearing Victorian-era scrapbook pages are a good example of 19th century folk art—an early form of collage.

Brand names on trade cards included Ivorine soap (the father of modern day Ivory soap); Muzzy's corn starch; Ball's corsets; Willimantic thread; J. S. Brownell butter, cheese, and eggs; Haines Brothers upright pianos; and Chase's liquid glue (used to glue the trade cards into scrapbooks).

Cigar-Store Indians

Besides flat, two-dimensional advertising, three-dimensional statues and carvings were also used to attract customers. The most common of these was the cigar-store Indian. Usually a little smaller than life size, these were expertly hand-carved and painted figures of Native Americans. The figures often held a carved pouch of tobacco or handful of cigars. The presence of a cigar-store Indian in front of a store told the customer that cigars and tobacco were sold there. Figures of were both male and female Indians were made. They usually featured a quite serious expression on their faces. Some had elaborate headdresses; others wore tobacco leaves on their heads.

The most well-known carvers of cigar-store Indians were brothers named Samuel and Charles Robb, whose New York City shop turned out hundreds of Indians between the 1870s and 1900. Cigar-store Indians are one of the most highly prized types of folk art, and the best of them sell for a small fortune today.

Trade Signs

A perfect example of public folk art is trade signs. In the days long before neon lights and factory-printed signs, people who were in business relied upon handmade, hand-painted signs to advertise their trades. Even the simplest of these signs are highly valued as folk art today. Most were just words stencil-painted onto wooden signs. The best of these signs are the ones that have detailed descriptions of stores and what was being offered for sale. One 1870s store had a series of signs that offered "Tin, wooden-ware, cutlery, tea-trays, and house-keeping articles." Imagine ten buildings on a block, each with that many signs. On a crowded 19th-century city street, a pedestrian could easily be overwhelmed by all the trade signs competing with each other for attention.

Drugstore Trade Signs

Drugstore trade sign from Illinois, early 20th century.

Trade signs used recognizable symbols that people would instantly understand. Many trade signs used symbols that you can still find today, such as the familiar looking pharmacist's mortar and pestle. These basic tools have been used for thousands of years. They were used by druggists of days past to mix ingredients and make medications for their customers.

A lot has changed in a hundred years. Drugstores used to be places where you could have a drink, make a telephone call, and get all kinds of strange remedies and concoctions, as well as more common items. Today, many drugs have brand names, but back then, drugs were simply known by their chemical names. Pharmacists were experts in the mixing of different chemicals and substances. The wrong mixture could spell disaster—a fiery explosion.

The mortar and pestle displayed in drugstore trade signs represent not only the grinding of solid ingredients to make powder, but the mixing of chemicals in general, both liquid and solid. The symbol was supposed to make the customer confident that in this store, there was an expert who could make any concoction under the sun.

Below is an actual list of some of the items sold by a New York drugstore in the spring of 1905. How many of these items can you find in your household today? If you don't know what something is, ask a parent or grandparent. Some things are simpler than they sound, for example, a bronchial lozenge is the equivalent of today's cough drop. Pretend you are a drugstore owner who is painting a special sign advertising low prices for 5 of these items.

MATERIALS

Sheet of white cardstock paper
at least 8½ by 11 inches

Markers or paints

Draw or paint your drugstore's name at the top of the sign. Next, select five items from the list below that you want to advertise. Which items do you think would be most popular with drugstore customers back in 1905? Use your imagination to letter the items and their prices per unit (gallon, pound, etc). Be creative in your design with colors and style of lettering.

Almond meal	Insect exterminator
Ammonia	Licorice candy
Axalic acid	Lime drops
Bandage	Linseed oil
Benzine	Malted milk
Bicarbonate of soda	Moth balls
Bismuth	Mustard leaves
Borax	Mustard plaster
Boric acid	Oil cedar
Bronchial lozenges	Ointment
Caffeine powder	Phenacetin
Camphor	Quinine
Carbolic acid	Sanitol
Carlsbad salt	Seidlitz powder
Castor oil	Syringe
Cotton	Syrup of figs
Epsom salt	Tablets
Essence of ginger	Talcum
Essence of peppermint	Tar balls
Florida water	Toilet paper
Fly paper	Toothbrush
French chalk	Turpentine
Gauze	White Vaseline
Hoffman's drops	Witch hazel

Also considered valuable and interesting today are signs that were carved or shaped to match a person's occupation, such as that of a boot for a shoemaker. These types of signs were very useful, because even if a person could not read, he or she knew what the store was. A sign featuring an elephant wearing boots was offered at a major auction house, with an estimated value of $30,000 to $50,000.

Old red-and-white barber poles are also highly prized today, though most people have no idea what the poles symbolize. Hundreds of years ago, barbers had more than one job. In addition to cutting hair and shaving faces, they also performed surgery or did a bloodletting using leeches. The red on the pole represents the bloody rags that sopped up the patients' wounds; the white represents the clean bandages, and the pole represents the pole that the patients held onto while being "treated."

How did business owners find a sign maker? Through word-of-mouth, or by checking their local newspaper's classified advertisements. For example, two sign painters advertised their skills in the May 31, 1834, edition of the *New York Sun*: Victor D. A. Browere's ad reads "Sign and Ornamental Painter, no. 203 Bowery," and Jarvis F. Hanks's ad proclaims, "Sign painting, in all its variety done in the neatest manner." To make sure nobody would ever have trouble finding him, Mr. Browere paid for his ad to appear in the paper every day for a full year!

Building Signs

In addition to displaying the usual hanging wood or metal trade signs, shop and business owners in cities and towns sometimes thought on a bigger scale. Many businesses paid for advertisements and signs to be painted directly on the sides of brick and stone buildings, which were usually 3 to 10 stories tall and next to either a vacant lot or a shorter building. Taller buildings of 20 and 30 stories that were built during the 1920s and 1930s might have a featured cascade of different signs painted from top to bottom. These hand-painted signs told pedestrians where to find the shop and what kind of goods or services were sold there. Every type of business, from hotels to dressmaking shops to restaurants advertised in this way, mostly between the late 1800s and the mid-1900s.

The signs were painted by people who were hired by sign companies. Nicknamed "wall dogs," these itinerant painters worked at dangerous heights, mixed their own paints, and made an advertisement come to life in giant proportions. It took many days and much hard work to paint the largest of these signs. Some of the boldest surviving building signs are for Omega Oil. This medicinal product advertised its cure for "weak backs" on a large scale. One bright blue sign stretches four stories high across three buildings (see photo on page 106). Each building used for a building sign was a different size and shape, so designing and executing each ad was a challenge. Their uniqueness is part of what makes them folk art.

Omega Oil signs painted on three buildings, early 20th century.

As buildings are demolished in cities today, very old building signs that have been hidden from view by nearby structures emerge again, sometimes 50 or more years after being covered up. Unfortunately, many are soon covered up again when new construction begins next door.

Faded signs still exist that explain where to buy tickets for the next steamer (a steam-powered ship that crossed the ocean—the only way to get to Europe before the jet age). There are also signs left for a laxative called Castoria. These signs date back to the 1910s to 1920s. There are even a few signs from the 1870s and 1880s still in existence, including some that advertise horse-drawn carriages.

Building signs are still occasionally painted these days, but new technology now allows them to be digitally printed, with no help from "wall dogs" required.

Tavern and Inn Signs

Long before the first 24-hour convenience store, all-night diner, or hotel there were taverns and inns. These types of establishments were common in pre-20th-century Europe, and they were recreated in America by the first colonists. On pitch-dark, windy nights, life thrived in the tavern. Drink and food could be had late into the evening. Even the otherwise strict Puritans of 18th-century New England enjoyed drinking in taverns. Travelers who stopped in for a rest entertained the others with stories, and the local townspeople shared news and gossip. A fireplace warmed the night to refresh the cold and weary visitors, and laughter filled the dense, smoky air. Patrons puffed happily on long-stemmed clay pipes while enjoying their evening.

Naturally, people traveling from another town wanted to know which building was the tavern. Many looked like ordinary houses, and some taverns were in fact part of houses. In various places, laws were passed requiring taverns and inns to place a sign outside their establishments that made it easier for travelers to locate them.

Often made by the same traveling artists who did stenciling in peoples' homes, these signs featured pictures of animals and people, along with the name of the establishment. For example, the Bull's Head Tavern might have featured a bull's

Activity

Pick Your Trade

Having a trade sign was a good way to attract customers to a shop. The larger, more colorful, or more dramatic a sign was, the better it attracted customers. In this activity you will try your hand at making a trade sign.

MATERIALS

Large letter stencils (available at a craft store)

Stencil brush or stencil sponge

Poster paints or acrylic paints of various colors (water soluble)

Foam board, at least 15 by 20 inches

Paintbrush

Exacto knife (adult supervision required)

First, decide what business you want to advertise on your sign. It can be either a modern business or an old-time business. Some possible choices include: barber, blacksmith, lawyer, doctor, music teacher, piano tuner, printer, furniture maker, grocer, printer, tailor or seamstress, detective, and tanner.

Use the stencils to paint words that relate to your business onto the foam board and paint decorations on the sign. Cut the board into a shape if you want to, but if you use an Exacto knife, ask an adult to help you.

Use your imagination to come up with an interesting sign. For example, if you wanted to make a podiatrist's, or foot doctor's, sign, you could paint a footprint or two on it. For a shoemaker's sign, you could cut the board into the shape of a shoe. For a music teacher's sign, you could cut the board into the shape of a violin.

head, while the Royal Tavern might have shown a crown or a lion, symbols of royalty. One of the few known inn-sign painters was William Rice (1777–1847), who painted at least 20 different signs in Connecticut. Rice favored using eagles and lions on his signs.

Of the tens of thousands of tavern and inn signs that were painted in the 18th and 19th centuries, only a fraction still exist today.

Roadside America

Old trade and tavern signs were meant to draw in people who traveled by horse and carriage or by foot. During the 1930s and 1940s, however, the automobile exploded in popularity. Planners all across the country realized that the existing roads were not adequate to handle the new automobile traffic. In addition, there were no big roads that linked major cities together. It was then that the first freeways, expressways, and highways were created.

A new form of the trade sign began to pop up along the side of the road—the billboard. Unlike the trade sign or building sign, the billboard often advertised an attraction that was many miles down the road. Some billboards were placed in series to keep reminding the driver where to go. "Sleepy Mountain Lodge, don't stop now, 10 miles ahead!" a sign might read, followed by "Sleepy Mountain Lodge, rest awaits, only 5 miles ahead!" and then "Sleepy Mountain Lodge, get the best night's rest just 1 mile ahead on the left!"

In addition to billboards, other forms of roadside advertising were devised between the

Building art over a doorway, early 20th century.

Murals, Frescoes, and Building Decorations

Not all public folk art was made for advertising purposes. Some was meant to be purely decorative. The early 20th century saw an explosion in the popularity of carved stone and wood figures on buildings. They sprang up everywhere—over doorways, under windows, and on the corners of buildings. Many early figures were inspired by Gothic figures of the Renaissance, but in the 20th century, the art form took a new direction toward folk art.

Some buildings that are still standing today feature dozens of odd-looking carvings. These carvings range from scary gnomes that look like they are ready to leap off the building, to beautiful mythological figures, brave-looking soldiers, and ordinary folks. One can only guess at what some of these building statues were meant to represent. A perfect example is the colorful doorway artwork shown here that depicts a man working by candlelight. What might have this figure symbolized?

In addition to exterior building art, murals and frescoes were painted on the interior walls and ceilings of some public and private buildings. "Mural painting" is the art of painting scenes directly onto dry walls. "Fresco painting" is the art of painting on fresh wet plaster with paint that is mixed with water. Only wealthy people could afford to have frescoes or murals. The late 19th century was known as the Gilded Age because of all the newly created industrial-age wealth. It was a boom time for mansion building, and all kinds of artisans were needed on such projects.

1930s and 1950s. As more Americans took to the roads, business owners knew it would take more than a common sign to attract the occupants of these speeding vehicles. Entire buildings were built in odd shapes as a way to attract business. In 1931, a duck farmer on Long Island, New York, built a 20-foot-high building shaped like a duck, from where he sold duck eggs. Known as the Big Duck, the building is still standing and is used to sell souvenirs today.

A German immigrant named Hermann Albrecht (1854–1916) was one New York City fresco painter who was hired to paint colored ceiling ornamentation and moldings in the mansions of the rich and famous, including those of the industrialist Gould family and the banker J. P. Morgan (1837–1913). Employment for most fresco and mural artists was spotty, however, they were sometimes unemployed for weeks or months at a time. Since fresco and mural painting were not so commonly done, it is likely that these artists also spent some time doing ordinary house painting for extra money.

Once the Great Depression hit in 1929, the mansion-building boom was finished. However, during the Depression, President Franklin Roosevelt created a program called the WPA (Works Progress Administration) that funded writers and artists. The Artists Project, a division of the WPA employed 1,500 artists across the country. Some of the best murals that exist today were painted by artists from that era who otherwise might have been unemployed. These mural paintings were done in schools and other public places to serve as a morale booster to both the artists, who were employed, and the viewing public, which was inspired and awed by the monumental works of art that focused on the power of everyday people to make America a better place.

Patriotic advertisement, late 19th century.

Patriotic Items

Ever since the Revolutionary War, Americans have been demonstrating their love of their country with red, white, and blue flags, posters, plaques, statues, stitched samplers, and many other unique items.

Patriotic art is public art, made to show pride in the country, and often made to be displayed for all to see. Unlike a lot of other kinds of folk art,

Folk Art

The urge to create is very strong among people across the world, and it all starts in childhood. Some of the greatest works of folk art were created not by adults, but by children. Because kids are highly creative and inventive, they are a natural fit for the freedom of folk art. Much of the 18th and 19th century crafts and artworks created by children are now considered folk art.

Among the works made by children include samplers (almost all of them were made by young girls), embroidery, coverlets, models, drawings, and paintings (including mourning pictures). The best adult folk artists are able to stay in touch with their "inner child," which allows them to create the same primitive work that a kid would make.

The sketch shown here was made by a young girl during World War I. Perhaps it is a drawing of her father or brother, or maybe a friend of the family who was in the navy. This old piece of art, on a yellowing piece of paper, still feels relevant today because kids around the country continue to have family members who are serving in the armed forces and who are exposed to danger on a daily basis.

Drawing of a sailor by eight-year-old Sara Gorton, 1918.

by Kids

however, patriotic art is made to evoke a strong emotional response in its viewer. It is created using a few common themes, including the flag, the eagle, Uncle Sam, the Statue of Liberty, and George Washington. American patriotic art has a homegrown quality to it that qualifies it as folk art. It is usually very vibrant, and it is often created in bursts during critical times in history, such as World War I or World War II.

The Civil War inspired patriotic art on both sides—Union and Confederacy. An 1871 advertisement praises an eye-tricking engraving of the United States Constitution that, when looked at from a distance, reveals the portraits of "Grant!! Sherman! Sheridan! Meade! and Thomas!"—all Civil War Union generals. "The whole is encompassed within a beautifully designed border of military emblems and scroll work."

Patriotic art often depicts things that are normally not found in any other type of artwork. A perfect example is a U.S. Army handkerchief that was made during World War II. It features illustrations of an anti-tank gun, soldiers, a jeep, a tank, searchlights, antiaircraft guns, and a motorcycle gun crew. The handkerchief is dedicated to "Mother," and it features this poem:

There's a dear little house inviting
In a dear little place I know
And a welcome is always waiting
When to that little house I go.
For there lives the dearest lady
The sweetest I ever met.
And to-day, if I cannot visit
Dear Mother, I don't forget.

Folk Art Survey

Folk art is all around us, whether in the city or country, on the East Coast or the West Coast. A survey of almost any neighborhood reveals weather vanes, whirligigs, murals or paintings on the outside of buildings, old trade signs, carved wood statues, hex signs, cast-iron doorstops, decorative flags and banners, patriotic art, and old barns.

The unlikely combination of guns blazing and sentimental words show how interesting patriotic art can be. Patriotic art has always been an outlet for national pride mixed with intense grief over a missing or dead loved one.

In the World War I memorial painting shown here, a soldier and a sailor play bugles while Miss Liberty holds the commemorative plaque that lists the names of 13 men who died during the war. At the bottom center the Statue of Liberty stands proudly. Underneath her is a quote from then-President Woodrow Wilson: "The world must be made safe for democracy." The artist is trying to say that these men did not die in vain; they died for a good reason. It was not an easy thing to convince Americans, who had entered the war reluctantly after more than two years of stalemate fighting had already gone by. Any hope that the victory would be easy was crushed by the 116,000 American deaths that occurred overseas between 1917 and 1918. Thousands of communities across the country created World War I monuments to honor those who served and died.

After September 2001, patriotic art again rose in popularity. This art included spontaneous tributes to the lost and large spray-painted flags on walls everywhere, including a railroad underpass. Someone made an American flag out of a section of wood fence and put it up in a town square. Kids in a New York suburb made a giant patchwork American flag quilt, with names of the victims on each square. One of the largest artistic tributes was in Union Square, not far from the site of the World Trade Center, where hundreds of people left

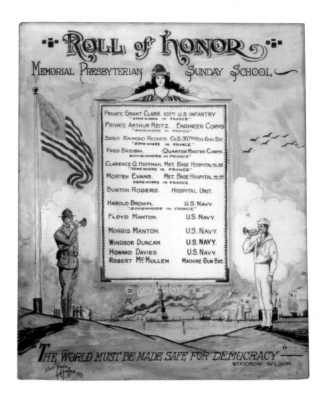

World War I memorial painting by
Charles Elmer Franklin, 1918.

mementos and created a living memorial. Not long after, city officials were unfortunately told to dismantle the impromptu memorial site, thus eliminating one of the most touching and spontaneous works of patriotic art ever created in this country.

Patriotic art turns up not only in every corner of this country, from Alaska to Arkansas, from North Dakota to New Mexico—it can also be found in practically every country in the world, from Albania to Zaire.

Folk art is more popular today than ever. Thanks to shows such as the *Antiques Roadshow*, millions of Americans across the country have been exposed to folk art for the first time. Artists young and old continue to find inspiration in the beauty of America. Since Grandma Moses and Howard Finster, more attention is being paid these days to folk artists while they are still alive. Many folk artists are very busy sharing their art. Living folk artists such as Mr. Imagination are traveling across the country doing workshops to teach kids how to make art, and cultivating relationships with authors, galleries, and museums.

While American folk art was barely of interest to many people just 100 years ago, there are now books on almost every imaginable type of folk art. Anyone can pick up a book and learn about making baskets, creating mosaics, building model warships, collecting cloth dolls, decorating Easter eggs, making quilts, creating hooked rugs, and much more.

Many current American folk artists continue to paint the themes and styles that were popular during the 19th century, using a pleasant primitive perspective. Popular subjects are farms, animals, and landscapes. Some living folk artists grew up at a time when most of the country was still rural, and they paint their memories of childhood. Other current artists use old pieces of furniture, scraps of tin, slate, or old buckets to make beautiful primitive-style folk art pieces. New self-taught artists continue to be "discovered" across the country by delighted folk art lovers.

Folk art is not stuck in one time period or style. New folk expressions continue to be inspired by the events of the world. It is easy to say that folk art will continue for as long as ordinary people continue to experiment with their creativity. But the real question is, what will the folk art of the future look like?

As the world continues to become more ethnically mixed, American folk art will become more and more diverse. Just as the German immigrants of the 18th century brought with them traditions of Fraktur, future immigrants will influence American art and design of the future.

People in the future could become very interested in the ways of the past and create a revival in crafts such as embroidery and tramp art. Or maybe much of the folk art of the future will be completely digital, created on computers and uploaded onto Web sites. Or maybe it will be holographic, projected three-dimensionally into the air. Perhaps new kinds of paint will be invented. As people develop new ways to be creative, it's guaranteed that folk art will follow those new paths.

The best thing about folk art is that anyone can make it. Folk art is made with love and some creativity. And that is truly a great combination.

Folk Art Now
Afterword

Glossary

Academic painting: A painting done by a professionally trained artist who has connections in the art world.

Amish: "Plain" people of German ancestry who do not believe in technology, and who live mainly in Pennsylvania and Ohio.

Art brut: A "raw" type of folk art that can be very emotional and surreal.

Assemblage: A gathering of different items used to make a three-dimensional work of art.

Calligraphy: Careful and elaborate writing or drawing, using a calligraphy pen and a bottle of ink.

Cigar-store Indian: A carved and painted wooden Indian figure that was placed in front of a shop to let people know cigars and tobacco were sold there.

Collage: An artwork that uses a variety of different materials, including found objects. It can be either two- or three-dimensional.

Daguerreotype: An early form of photograph, it spelled the end for folk portrait painting.

Decorative arts: The decoration of plain, everyday objects with painted designs.

Decoupage: Decorating a practical object, such as a bowl or box, with artfully arranged and glued pieces of paper.

Decoy: A fake duck or fish, made of wood, and used by hunters to attract the real thing.

Distelfink: The German word for the thistle finch, a common subject in Pennsylvania Dutch art.

Embroidery: The art of sewing colored threads onto fabric to create designs.

Flemish art: A nickname for pyrography that comes from the name of the company that popularized the hobby.

Found objects: Old or new junk, scraps, or odds and ends that are found anywhere and recycled for use in art.

Fraktur: A German and German-American style of drawing letters and decorations using colorful brush and pen strokes. Common themes include tulips and angels.

Fresco painting: The art of painting designs and decoration on wet plaster.

Grain painting: Painting cheap wood with sponges and combs to create the appearance of expensive wood.

Hex: A colorful circular sign that features geometric patterns, such as stars, rosettes, or other designs.

Hooked rug: A rug made from scraps of fabric that are pulled through the holes in a piece of burlap and knotted.

Illuminated manuscript: A colorful, hand-lettered, designed book dating to the 16th century and earlier.

Itinerant: A person who travels from place to place looking for work.

Japanning: Placing a black coating on top of tin to create a uniform surface to paint designs onto.

Landscape: A painting that features outdoor scenery.

Limner: A folk portrait painter.

Marquetry: The art of laying thin strips of wood next to each other to create a patchwork appearance of different colors and grains.

Mennonites: A religious group that came to the United States in the 1680s, similar to the Amish in some beliefs.

Mixed media: Using two or more different kinds of decoration, for example, paint and pencil or pastels and ink.

Model: An object, such as a car, boat, or house, that is made in miniature form. Folk artists use scraps and found objects to make their models.

Mural painting: The art of creating large, sometimes epic paintings directly onto walls.

Outsider: An artist who works outside the regular art world.

Pennsylvania Dutch: People in certain counties in central and eastern Pennsylvania who are descended from the German immigrants who arrived in the 18th century.

Poker art: An early name for pyrography, given because people used to use red-hot pokers to burn designs onto wood.

Primitive: A term applied to any artwork that is done in a rustic or childlike method that can be simple in style, yet very detailed.

Provenance: The history of a piece of folk art, from its making all the way to the present, including who owned it and where they lived.

Pyrography: The art of burning a design into soft wood.

Quilt: A bed covering that is usually made with three layers: a bottom layer of fabric, a middle layer of stuffing, and a top layer that is made with different scraps of fabric sewn into a recognizable pattern.

Rag doll: A doll made with scraps of fabric and yarn.

Relief: A carving (usually stone, bone, or shell) that stands out three-dimensionally from a flat background.

Reward of merit: A hand-painted or colored certificate given to an exceptional student by his or her teacher.

Sampler: A stitched piece, made by schoolgirls, that usually features numbers and the alphabet.

Scherenschnitte: The art of decorative paper cutting.

Scrimshaw: The art of inscribing a design onto a tooth, a piece of ivory, or whale bone with a sharp instrument.

Shadow box: An open, shallow box filled with decorative items or figures to make a three-dimensional model or colorful display.

Shakers: A religious community, founded in the late 18th century, that believes in hard work and a simple life. They are known for their folk art baskets, boxes, and furniture.

Silhouette: A person's profile cut out of black paper as an inexpensive alternative to a painted portrait.

Slip: A slippery mix of water and clay that is used to coat pottery.

Spencerian: A method of calligraphy that inspired many elaborate ink drawings of birds and other animals.

Stencil: A cut-out design that can be held to a wall or other surface and painted over to create a design in that shape.

Stoneware: Durable pottery that is baked at high temperatures and is sometimes decorated with blue designs.

Theorem: A small painting made using stencils.

Toleware: Painted tinware that is usually coated black and then painted with colored leaf and flower designs.

Trade card: An early form of advertising that featured interesting color illustrations on a small collectible card.

Trade sign: A hand-painted shop sign, which was sometimes cut out into a trade-related shape, such as a boot.

Tramp art: Notch-carved wood that is made into picture frames, boxes, and other decorative items.

Trench art: Vases, letter openers, and other items made using scrap battlefield metal from bullets and shells.

Visionary art: A type of art that is created based on dreams and visions the artist has.

Wall dog: A painter who labored to decorate the sides of buildings with colorful advertisements.

Weather vane: A decorative metal object that indicates wind direction when mounted atop a building.

Whirligig: A wooden decorative object with parts that move with the wind.

Zanerian: A school of calligraphy that inspired fancy ink drawings.

American Folk Art Museum

45 West 53rd Street
New York, NY 10019
(212) 265-1040
This museum has an excellent collection of folk art, from fraktur to outsider art.
www.folkartmuseum.com

South Street Seaport Museum

207 Front Street
New York, NY 10038
(212) 748-8600
This museum focuses on the maritime history of New York City.
www.southstseaport.org

Historic Deerfield

Off Routes 5 and 10
Deerfield, MA 01342
(413) 774-5581
An entire village of 18th- and 19th-century houses filled with antiques and folk art can be found here.
www.historic-deerfield.org

Smithsonian Institution

The Mall
Washington, DC 20013
(202) 357-2700
This is a repository for the nation's treasures, including antiques and folk art.
www.si.edu

High Museum Folk Art and Photography Galleries

30 John Wesley Dobbs Avenue, NE
Atlanta, GA 30303
(404) 577-6940
The High Museum has an extensive folk art collection, and hosts numerous traveling exhibits each year.
www.high.org

Winterthur Museum

Route 52 (Kennett Pike)
Winterthur, DE 19735
(800) 448-3883
One of the best collections of American art and antiques in the country is found here.
www.winterthur.org

Henry Ford Museum and Greenfield Village

20900 Oakwood Boulevard
Dearborn, MI 48124
(313) 982-6100
This museum has an extensive collection of Americana, including folk art.
www.hfmgv.org

John Michael Kohler Arts Center

608 New York Avenue
Sheboygan, WI
(920) 458-4473
In addition to its impressive collection, this museum is actively involved in the preservation and restoration of folk art environments around the United States.
www.jmkac.org

Old Sturbridge Village

1 Old Sturbridge Village Road
Sturbridge, MA 01566
(508) 347-3362
See a restoration of an old Massachusetts village.
www.osv.org

Sabbathday Lake Shaker Village Museum and Library

707 Shaker Road
New Gloucester, ME 04260
(207) 926-4597
Learn more about the Shakers at the site of the only active Shaker community left in the country.
www.shaker.lib.me.us

Pennsylvania Farm Museum

2451 Kissel Hill Road
Lancaster, PA 17601
(717) 569-0401
This museum features an excellent collection of Pennsylvania Dutch artifacts.
www.landisvalleymuseum.org

Kentucky Folk Art Center

102 West First Street
Morehead, KY 40351
(606) 783-2204
This museum focuses on the traditional and visionary folk art of eastern Kentucky and Appalachia.
www.kyfolkart.org

Museums
with Folk Art Collections

Cold Spring Harbor Whaling Museum
Main Street
Cold Spring Harbor, NY 11724
(613) 367-3418
Preserving the legacy of whaling in this former hub of whaling activity, this museum features numerous scrimshaw items.
www.cshwhalingmuseum.org

Shelburne Museum
U.S. Route 7
Shelburne, VT 05482
(802) 985-3346
Here's another good location to view folk art.
www.shelburnemuseum.org

New York Historical Society
2 West 77th Street
New York, NY 10024
(212) 873-3400
One of New York's finest historical collections is found here.
www.nyhistory.org

Abby Aldrich Folk Art Museum
Colonial Williamsburg
Williamsburg, VA 23187
(800) HISTORY
One of the best collections of folk art in the country is housed here. Within Colonial Williamsburg, there are also numerous 18th-century buildings that contain antiques and folk art.
www.history.org/history/museums/abby_art.cfm

American Visionary Art Museum
800 Key Highway
Baltimore, MD 21230
(410) 244-1900
This museum features the work of outsider artists.
www.avam.org

Shaker Museum and Library
88 Shaker Museum Road
Old Chatham, NY 12136
(518) 794-9100
Founded in 1950, this is the first public museum dedicated to preserving the life and art of the Shakers. Its collection totals 18,500 objects.
www.shakermuseumoldchat.org

Museum of International Folk Art
706 Camino Lejo
Santa Fe, NM 87504
(505) 827-6350
This museum has more the 125,000 objects from more than a hundred countries, as well as the United States, in its collection.
www.moifa.org

Enfield Shaker Museum
24 Caleb Dyer Lane
Enfield, NH 03748
(603) 632-4346
Dedicated to preserving the history of Enfield Shaker Village, this museum also offers craft workshops.
www.shakermuseum.org

Fayette Art Museum
530 North Temple Avenue
Fayette, AL 35555
(205) 932-8727
This museum's 3,500-work collection focuses on Southern folk artists.

Museum of the American Indian
Smithsonian Institution
One Bowling Green
New York, NY 10004
(212) 514-3700
This museum features the art of the native peoples of North, Central, and South America.
www.si.edu/nmai

New York State Historical Association
Fenimore House
Cooperstown, NY 13326
(607) 547-1421
This is a good place to see beautiful works of folk art.
www.nysha.org

The Mariners Museum
100 Museum Drive
Newport News, VA 23606
(757) 596-2222
Maritime-related art is showcased here.
www.mariner.org

Schwenkfelder Library and Heritage Center
105 Seminary Street
Pennsburg, PA 18073
(215) 679-3103
A center devoted to the culture and art of the Schwenkfelder religious group, which is especially known for its gorgeous frakturs.
www.schwenkfelder.com

Mennello Museum of American Folk Art
900 East Princeton Street
Orlando, FL 32803
(417) 246-4279
This museum features the works of Earl Cunningham (1893~1977).
www.mennellomuseum.com

San Francisco Craft and Folk Art Museum
Building A, Fort Mason Center
Laguna and Marina Boulevard
San Francisco, CA 94123
This museum has no permanent collection, but an active program of changing exhibits.
www.sfcaftandfolk.org

Selected Bibliography and Further Reading

All of these books have illustrations and are therefore suitable for all ages.

Bacon, Lenice Ingram. *American Patchwork Quilts*. New York: William Morrow & Company, 1973.

Baird, Ljiljana. *Quilts*. Philadelphia, PA: Courage Books, 1994.

Bassett, Lynne Z., and Jack Larkin. *Northern Comfort: New England's Early Quilts, 1780–1850*. Nashville, TN: Rutledge Hill Press, 1998.

Bishop, Adele, and Cile Lord. *The Art of Decorative Stenciling*. New York: Viking Press, 1976.

Black, Mary, and Jean Lipman. *American Folk Painting*. New York: Clarkson N. Potter, Inc., 1966.

Bowman, Doris M. *The Smithsonian Treasury—American Quilts*. Washington, DC: Smithsonian Institution Press, 1991.

Edwards, Sybil, Chris Moore, and Lynette Bleiler. *Decorative Folk Art: Exciting Techniques to Transform Everyday Objects*. Devon, UK: David and Charles, 1996.

Fendelman, Helaine, and Jonathan Taylor. *Tramp Art: A Folk Art Phenomenon*. New York: Stewart, Tabori & Chang, 1999.

Fjelstul, Alice Bancroft, and Patricia Brown Schad with Barbara Marhoefer. *Early American Wall Stencils in Color*. New York: E.P. Dutton, 1982.

Harris, David. *The Art of Calligraphy: A Practical Guide to the Skills and Techniques*. New York: DK Publishing, Inc., 1995.

Hechtlinger, Adelaide. *American Quilts, Quilting, & Patchwork: The Complete Book of History, Technique & Design*. New York: Galahad Books, 1974.

Hollander, Stacy, and Brooke Davis Anderson. *American Anthem: Masterworks from the American Folk Art Museum*. New York: Harry N. Abrams, 2001.

Ketchum, William C., Jr. *American Folk Art*. New York: Todtri Productions Limited, 1995.*

Ketchum, William C., Jr. *The Pottery and Porcelain Collector's Handbook*. New York: Funk and Wagnalls, 1971.*

Ketchum, William C., Jr. *American Pottery and Porcelain*. New York: Black Dog and Leventhal Publishers, 2000.*

Lipman, Jean, and Alice Winchester. *The Flowering of American Folk Art (1776–1876)*. New York: Viking Press, 1974.

Lipman, Jean, and Tom Armstrong, eds. *American Folk Painting of Three Centuries*. New York: Hudson Hills Press, Inc., 1980.

Malley, Richard C. *In Their Hours of Leisure: Scrimshaw in the Cold Spring Harbor Whaling Museum*. Cold Spring Harbor, NY: Whaling Museum Society, 1993.

Pollak, Jane. *Decorating Eggs: Exquisite Designs with Wax and Dye*. New York: Sterling Publishing, Inc., 1996.

Polley, Robert L., ed. *Treasures of American Folk Arts and Crafts in Distinguished Museums and Collections*. New York: G.P. Putnam's Sons, 1968.

Various authors. *Americana: Folk and Decorative Art*. New York: Roundtable Press, Inc., 1982.

Various authors. *Self-taught Artists of the 20th Century*. San Francisco, CA: Chronicle Books, 1998.

Wertkin, Gerard C. *The Four Seasons of Shaker Life: An Intimate Portrait of the Community at Sabbathday Lake*. New York: Fireside Books, 1986.

Yoder, Don, and Thomas E. Graves. *Hex Signs: Pennsylvania Dutch Barn Symbols and Their Meaning*. Mechanicsburg, PA: Stackpole Books, 2000.

*Author's note: William Ketchum has written many more wonderful books on folk art, any of which would be fine reading on the subject.

Index